'Two years in a Russian prison have made Pussy Riot activist Maria Alyokhina more determined than ever to protest against Vladimir Putin's regime . . . Alyokhina's fight to improve the brutal conditions at the camps is the fulcrum of her book . . . the literary equivalent of guerrilla street art' Marc Bennetts, *The Times*

'An energetic and enjoyable prison diary . . . A search for meaningful protest in an age in which presidents often appear to be playful performance artists . . . joining in the grand tradition of prison experiences' Peter Pomerantsev, *Spectator*

'Alyokhina's eye for surreal detail gives *Riot Days* a welcome dose of dark humour . . . Through the chinks in the abusive system, Alyokhina glimpses human beings' Sophie Pinkham, *The New York Times Book Review*

'In oppressive political systems, some of the most effective weapons are sarcasm and dark humour. It is exactly these weapons that are employed by Masha Alyokhina in the brilliantly written *Riot Days*. Once you begin reading, you are completely disarmed, unable to put it down until the last page' Marina Abramovic

'A women's prison memoir like no other! One tough cookie!' @MargaretAtwood

'Strong, brave, honest, touching, bitter and sad' Vladimir Sorokin, master of contemporary Russian literature

'A punk call to arms . . . whose work hauntingly reminds us to never stop fighting for democracy, even if we feel complacent within our current society's embrace' *Dazed*

'Riot Days could so easily have been a straightforward, from-the-horse's-mouth confessional account of one of the most publicised political protests of recent years. Alyokhina takes on a far greater challenge: creating a piece of art in itself' Rachel Hewitt, *Guardian*

'*Riot Days*, her debut book/punk manifesto, vividly recounts her arrest, trial and imprisonment with the same urgency that fuels Pussy Riot, juxtaposing diary extracts, graffiti doodles, court transcripts, song lyrics and newspaper accounts with the author's own laser-sharp reflections on protest, censorship, art, freedom and religion' *Big Issue*

ABOUT THE AUTHOR

Maria Alyokhina is a political activist, artist and member of Pussy Riot collective. After 'Punk Prayer' – a Pussy Riot performance of the song 'Mother Mary, banish Putin' in Moscow Cathedral on 21 February 2012 she was convicted of 'hooliganism motivated by religious hatred', sentenced for two years' imprisonment and transported to a penal colony in the Urals, one of the hardest prison systems in the world. As a political prisoner she campaigned to improve the lives of her fellow inmates in the penal colony and continued her work as an activist and artist outside. She is a co-founder of the independent Russian media outlet MediaZona and actor with the Belarus Free Theatre.

Riot Days

MARIA ALYOKHINA

PENGUIN BOOKS

PENGUIN BOOKS

UK | USA | Canada | Ireland | Australia
India | New Zealand | South Africa

Penguin Books is part of the Penguin Random House group of companies
whose addresses can be found at global.penguinrandomhouse.com.

Penguin
Random House
UK

First published by Allen Lane 2017
Published in Penguin Books 2018
002

Copyright © Maria Alyokhina, 2017

The moral rights of the authors and translator have been asserted

Set in 10.23/14 pt Warnock Pro
Typeset by Jouve (UK), Milton Keynes
Printed and bound in Great Britain by Clays Ltd, Elcograf S.p.A.

A CIP catalogue record for this book is available from the British Library

ISBN: 978-0-141-98661-6

Contents

Neither Fish nor Fowl
('Neither cunt, nor the Red Army')
– Old Russian saying

0. Prologue

We came up with an idea to make a film about the revolution. A real movie that would be shown in every theatre. Filming a frozen chicken being pushed up a cunt was good, but it wasn't for a mass audience. Art for the masses is made in Hollywood. Revolution requires a big screen.

We visited at least twenty studios during one week: identical offices, snow-white smiles. Getting appointments was easy for us – we were stars in all the newspapers.

'We want to make a movie about revolution.'
'Which revolution might that be?'
'The Russian revolution.'
'What do you mean? The 1917 Revolution?'
'No! The one that's happening now.'
'But there is no revolution now.'

Oh, really?
Perfect teeth. Suntanned bodies. Morning runs in sneakers.

'We'll buy your story if you're selling it.'
'But what about the revolution?'

1. My First Business

The summer was over. Darkness fell early. Putin announced he would run for a third presidential term.

The magical winter of 2011. The Snow Revolution. What will they write about it in the history books? Will they mention it at all? What will become of it – will it be the beginning of a bigger revolution that lies ahead? We were led by a belief in the possibility of change – a naive and childish belief that can awaken suddenly in adults, and is usually accompanied by feelings of shame and the need to justify oneself. We went out into the streets. We wrote and, letter by letter, we became a revolutionary statement. We wore white ribbons.

revolutionary writing

That winter, the little grey KGB agent Putin and a puffed-up, toy-like Medvedev decided to trade places: prime minister for president. Or maybe one of them decided – who cares? They called it 'castling', two pieces moving on the chessboard at the same time. They falsified the results of the elections to the Duma.

We believed that, if we pricked his ass with a pin, Putin would jump out of his presidential seat. He would leap up, and run to hell. His fleshy, Botoxed cheeks would head for the hills and roll off into the dustbin of history.

anyone can be pussy riot

I began to stay at the Bass Player's place, and joked about academia. 'It's rotten and mildewed,' I said. The Bass Player lived on the out-skirts of town in a tall building. In her apartment, there was a portrait of Beethoven and a faux-leopardskin blanket on the sofa. We talked until five in the morning and watched Pasolini movies a lot.

We loved only heroes. The 1968 student revolt in France, the Russian avant-garde in the early decades of the 20th century. At the same time, we were reading Alexander Vvedensky, a poet who was murdered by Stalin on a convoy somewhere between Kharkov and Kazan on its way to a penal colony. One weekend, I locked myself in the room where the Bass Player burned CDs. I was going to make a stencil for a T-shirt. I decided I had to make a revolutionary T-shirt. I didn't even notice when it got dark.

revolutionary t-shirt

When I went back out into the kitchen, it was full of girls. The Bass Player's floor was tiled in black and white squares, like a chessboard. The girls were wearing brightly coloured dresses. They were arguing so loudly it must have been audible two floors down.

'Check out the T-shirt I made,' I said. I was very proud of the first T-shirt I'd created myself.

'Céder un peu, c'est capituler beaucoup!'

'*Céder un peu, c'est capituler beaucoup!*' was stencilled on the T-shirt in black permanent marker. I had spent about five hours on it. The T-shirt was green. The girls were furiously cutting holes in colourful knitted balaclavas.

On the night of 4 December, there was a march along Chistye Prudy, past the FSB buildings, where prisoners are kept. Red fires from the flares. Temperature: 39°F. Wind: 5mph. Relative humidity: 88%. Haze. Arrests.

39°F, 5mph, 88%

The prisoners are hanging out a banner written with markers. Markers are banned in prison. They hang it up outside the bars, stretching their hands through the gaps. It reads: 'Judge Moskalenko – burn in HELL.'

The judge didn't burn in hell. She lives in it. She still works in the Russian court. The beginnings of the revolution's first large-scale street protest were underway. A really massive street protest, right by the Kremlin wall.

The riot police were in position. We entered Revolution Square, 10 December 2011.

you can't even imagine we exist

In January, we, Pussy Riot, started rehearsing in an old factory. After a while, the security guards were no longer surprised to see us. Oh, those girls are here again. Wearing strange-coloured tights, some weird headgear. Russia's a strange place, anyway. Katya said, 'It's odd that they never ask us any questions.' She thought there was something fishy about the way they let us come and go. But the security guards were just doing their job, drinking beer and watching TV.

> *'This is one of their whims. They send nine people to one place, twenty to another; in some countries, they don't think it's necessary to send any at all. If they want to teach something, they should teach their wives to make cabbage soup!'*
> – Vladimir Putin on European observers at Russian elections, 2008

little whims

You need at least one month of rehearsal to put an action together. When you go live, you only get one take.

You walk through a large hall in an old factory, put up a ladder, climb up on to the windowsill one by one. Shout out a song. 30, 40 times in a row.

get ready

With a large, heavy backpack, after every rehearsal, I took the last, nearly empty bus to the metro and jumped over the turnstile just in time to catch the train. I never had enough money to pay for the ride.

jump

The Kremlin is alarmed. The TV denies anything unusual is going on. *Condoms* – the word Putin used to describe the opposition's white ribbons. He meant that those who did not agree with him were just protection for a limp dick. Yeah, right.

putin peed his pants

The little towers of the Kremlin were dark; the snow was white. They used to execute people on Lobnoye Mesto.

On Lobnoye Mesto, there's a round stone platform that looks like an executioner's block. It's surrounded by stone walls that are maybe six feet high. It's like a large barrel cut in half. Inside, it can hold about thirty people.

In Red Square, directly facing the Kremlin.

The tsar read out decrees – *ukases* – here. And declared wars.

In 1968, eight dissidents climbed on to Lobnoye Mesto to protest against the invasion of Czechoslovakia.

for freedom – yours and mine

It was an unprecedented protest in Soviet Russia. The authorities responded with prison sentences and forced psychiatric treatment.

In the 1990s, Alexander Brener, an artist who had been incarcerated in a Dutch prison for drawing a dollar sign on a painting by Kazimir Malevich, hopped around Lobnoye Mesto in his underwear and boxing gloves. He shouted at the Kremlin, 'Come out, Yeltsin!'

Brener was called a 'hooligan' in the news. In 2000, Yeltsin resigned and made Putin president. Putin said, 'We need stability.' Stability was what he called himself.

floors swept, stability in place

When Pussy Riot performed on Lobnoye Mesto, we unfurled a violet flag: the Venus mirror symbol, a clenched fist in the centre. There were eight of us, like the eight dissidents in 1968.

revolution without caravaggio

As we were preparing for our Red Square action, Caravaggio's paintings were brought to Moscow. But it's not easy to carry a ladder into a museum. I didn't go to see the Caravaggio exhibition.

What a strange thing to be doing during the days of Russian Christmas, I thought, walking home through the woods after rehearsal.

At the rehearsal, smoke started billowing from the guitar amp. Katya rushed over and managed to fix it. She's an expert in nuclear submarines. And some of us couldn't even install a couple of editing apps on the computer.

'Smoke – that's cool!'

'We need smoke!'

'There's no smoke without fire!'

'Let's bring a poster and burn it!'

So, as well as singing 'Putin Peed His Pants', we decided to set fire to a poster of Putin kissing Qaddafi. We rehearsed the burning part for a long time: it was going to be cold, we'd have to douse the poster with kerosene. We gathered at the old factory in the evenings and practised burning the poster, day after day: unfold, douse, set alight, almost simultaneously.

learn how to burn it

A rebel column is marching on the Kremlin.
Windows of the FSB rooms are blowing out.
Bitches are shitting themselves behind red walls.
Riot announces, Abort the System!

Attack at dawn? I won't object.
For our freedom and yours I punish them with my lash.
The glorious Madonna will teach you how to fight.
The feminist Magdalene went to a protest march

Riot in Russia – charisma of protest!
Riot in Russia – Putin peed his pants!
Riot in Russia – we exist!
Riot in Russia – Riot, Riot!

Go out to the streets,
Live on the Red,
Show the freedom
Of civic anger.

Sick of the culture of male hysteria
The savage cult of the leader devours your brain
Orthodox religion of a hard penis
Patients are offered treatment by conformity

The regime is moving towards censoring dreams
It's about time for a clashing confrontation
A pack of bitches from the sexist regime
Beg forgiveness from the feminist fiends

Riot in Russia – charisma of protest!
Riot in Russia – Putin peed his pants!
Riot in Russia – we exist!
Riot in Russia – Riot, Riot!

Go out to the streets,
Live on the Red,
Show the freedom
Of civic anger.

the poster didn't catch fire

The cops got us afterwards for trespassing. We told them we were drama students. We said that we were staging a play and had decided to rehearse at Lobnoye Mesto. We gave them fake names. Actually, they were real names, just not our own: we'd taken them from the registry of traffic offenders, found people who matched our ages, used them as our own. False names. Done. It worked for everyone. Except me.

'Do you know you have an outstanding conviction?'
'Huh?'
'What's your name again?'
'Masha.' I had to come clean. That's how the police got hold of a copy of my passport. With my real address.

an outstanding conviction

I had never been in trouble with the police before. It had just never happened. I wasn't a revolutionary.

They hadn't heard 'Putin Peed His Pants'. The poster we'd failed to set alight came with us to the police station as evidence.

'If this is a play, what's Qaddafi got to do with it?' a policeman asked.
'Well, we just thought it was funny, so we printed it out.'

we printed out qaddafi

The cops bought that, too. We drank coffee from the machine, warmed ourselves, and laughed. The main thing was not to let them take the guitar – we didn't have money for a new one.

'Silly girls, you must be frozen,' the sergeant had said, while we were climbing down the stone walls of Lobnoye Mesto, which was covered with ice, in a torrent of snow. –12°F, relative humidity 85%.

You stand on the stone walls and it seems you'll fall any second. They are about ten feet high; but it isn't really about the height. You can't let yourself fall, because there won't be a second time.

We, Pussy Riot, went out to the square because we dreamed of a different history. Because the one in which the president turned into an emperor was not the one we desired. We were sick of lies. Of the unchanging, dismal lies broadcast on TV, the endless, groundless promises of a happy life.

a long and happy life

Riot is always a thing of beauty. That is how I got interested. At school, I had this dream of becoming a graffiti artist, and I practised graffiti in my school notepad. If you start your school work on the first page and do your sketches in the back, sooner or later the two will meet in the middle.

And, next to your history notes, graffiti appears.

Which turns history into a different story.

2. Pussy Riot Church

They are both former security agents, which is why they are in love with each other.

'Esteemed Vladimir Vladimirovich . . .'

'Thank you, Your Holiness.'

Putin, former KGB agent 'Mikhalych' and the Patriarch of All Russia, former KGB agent 'Mikhailov', are sitting in armchairs at a post-Christmas meeting. The Constitution decrees that Russia is a secular state, which means that Church and state are separate entities, they do not get involved in each other's affairs.

But these two would rather not talk about the Russian Constitution.

'As patriarch, I must speak only the truth and openly commend the enormous role that you, personally, Vladimir Vladimirovich, have played in correcting the crooked twist of our history.'

second coming, third term

Putin is getting ready for a third term. The patriarch sails off on a 680,000-dollar boat, while volunteers collect firewood for war veterans.

'You once said that you work for this country like a galley slave, but a galley slave makes no significant impact, while yours has been extremely effective.'

The institutions of power, the ruling party, and the Church, are servants of the tsar. You can't achieve any success in Russia if you are not enmeshed in this system.

But you can change the values, change the system.

change the system

The kitchen where we gathered after our Red Square action became our headquarters. We never mentioned addresses over the phone, because the lines were tapped by officers from the Centre for Combatting Extremism.

We ate whatever God sent our way, which was usually pasta.

After the meeting between Putin and the patriarch, it became clear that the patriarch was willing to use the Church to bolster any possible role the president might assume. He decided to put the Church at Putin's disposal, to lay it at his feet. To render Putin a demigod, not just a government official. His Holiness praised the past twelve years of Putin's rule as a 'miracle of God'.

The patriarch thanked Putin for their 'high level of agreement on the development of the spiritual, ethical, cultural, educational and other very important spheres in the life of our state'. And he went off to pose for photographs in his church with the Olympic team.

Following the trend, the Putin elite began showing off their spirituality. Are you going to church? You should take pictures while you're there. Their spirituality flashed brightest when the Holy Belt of the Virgin Mary was brought to the Cathedral of Christ the Saviour.

belt of the virgin mary

'Have you seen the pictures?'
'What pictures?'
'Of the belt.'
'The belt?'
'The Belt of the Virgin Mary.'

> *'Yes, cars drive up, and if they belong to state officials who are busy day and night thinking about the good of the people and who have no time to stand in line for hours, they might probably be let straight in to see the sacred relic. I don't see any crime in that.'*
> – A spokesman for Archpriest Mikhail Ryazantsev of the Cathedral of Christ the Saviour

vip pass

Government officials and other higher-ups got into the church cathedral with VIP passes. We looked at the pictures. They drove up in their Maybachs and kissed the belt. A done deal. No waiting in a queue for eight hours.

The church is no longer a place where everyone is equal.

CCS

In fact, it is not the Church that owns the building that houses the Cathedral of Christ the Saviour but the cathedral's foundation. And one of the foundation's board members is an official from the Ministry of the Interior: Vladimir Kolokoltsev: the Moscow police commissioner. And the private security services hired to guard the premises share his name: *kolokol*: meaning bell. Sounds like a joke.

For the right fee the church can provide:

Church service: $50
Corporate banquet: $970
Car wash: $100
Laundry and dry cleaning: $160

There are some things money can't buy. For everything else, there's the Cathedral of Christ the Saviour.

laundry-church

The church doesn't pay taxes; it sells fine porcelain eggs and custom-made replicas of imperial medals. You can order one for 500 bucks. You can also order a miniature copy of the church.

a $500 medal

A light machine; a sound machine; a soap-bubble machine; a snow machine; a heavy-fog machine; a light-fog machine. These are all for hire in the event halls of the cathedral. Because you're worth it.

All kind of things happen in this church that shouldn't. It's just another successful corporation.

> *'At present, there are no other large spaces in the capital that might be used for such community-church events.'*

actually – no

'Let's perform there.'
'In the church?'
'You call that a church?'
'In a *church*?'
'Sure.'

The kitchen door flew open. Petya rushed in; he had heard us from the next room.

'Do you know what the reaction will be?'
'What?'
'Hatred.'

I didn't believe in hate. No one believed in hate. 'Don't let the door hit you on the way out,' someone said to Petya. Nadya, I think.

We decided it was just the place.

virgin mary, banish putin

Virgin Mary, Mother of God, banish Putin!
Banish Putin, banish Putin!

Black cassocks, gold epaulettes
The parishioners all crawl and bow.
The ghost of freedom is in the heavens,
Gay Pride sent to Siberia in chains.

The head of the KGB, their chief saint,
Leads protesters to prison under escort.
So as not to offend the Most Sainted One,
Women must give birth and love.

Shit, shit, holy shit!
Shit, shit, holy shit!

Virgin Mary, Mother of God,
Be a feminist!
Be a feminist!

Bless our festering bastard-bosses.
Let black cars parade the cross.
The missionary's in class for cash,
Meet him there, and pay his stash

Patriarch Gundiai believes in Putin.
It'd be better to believe in God, you bitch!
The Belt of the Virgin won't deter the demonstrations.
The Virgin Mary is with us at the protests.

Virgin Mary, Mother of God, banish Putin, banish Putin!
Virgin Mary, Mother of God, banish Putin!

pussy riot church

We rehearsed for a long time. Every day for about a month. At an art gallery surrounded by a large park with benches. It was cold, and I was wearing my grandma's coat, which had huge shoulders. A badass military officer in a badass Cossack's hat. I loved it! It wasn't that I didn't have regular clothes, I just liked dressing that way.

'And so, Nadya Tolokonnikova, Ekaterina Samutsevich, Maria Alyokhina, and undetermined other persons, at a place and time also undetermined by the investigation, but no later than 17 February 2012, in circumstances undetermined by the investigation, entered into a criminal conspiracy.'

criminal conspiracy

The night before arrived. We agreed to meet the following morning, 21 February, 9 a.m., at Kropotinskaya station. I couldn't sleep that night. I was chatting with the Bass Player, who was coming, too. The closer Day X came, the more I questioned my right to do what we planned to do. I tried to make sense of it from a religious perspective. I asked the Bass Player, do I have the right to do this? Maybe I'm just a barbarian? She persuaded me that I most likely did have the right to do it – after all, 'you're not going to murder an old woman'. I definitely wasn't going there to kill anyone. I was going to the Cathedral of Christ the Saviour.

do I have the right?

'You have the right to do this,' the Bass Player said. And in the morning, she refused to go.

A February morning – gloomy, cloudy, cold. You don't want to go outside. It's not a winter's day, with snow crunching under your feet, or a day of spring sun, with a fresh wind and rivulets of melting ice gleaming on the asphalt. February is weird. Neither fish, nor fowl. Impossible to tell when the days begin, and when they end.

21/2/12

Music – I decided – would help me wake up. An old CD player and several CDs in the kitchen. I put the coffee on, inserted a CD, plugged in the player. The outlet exploded.

Naturally. It had to happen on this, of all days.

music and electricity

The kitchen, the hallway, the street, one metro stop after the other – after the electric shock I'd had, I saw all this through blurred vision and white splotches. I thought maybe I could catch some sleep on the train. I had a long way to go and had to change train, though I suspected that at this time of the morning the metro would be packed with people on their way to work. And it was. Jam packed. I was only able to sit down before my last stop, for all of two minutes.

transfer at lenin library station

Maybe I did sleep a bit. The dreams I had were also marked by white spots, like icy giraffes.

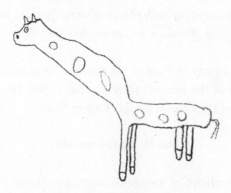

Serafima was the one I saw first. She was sitting on the ground, dozing by a huge column. Tiny Serafima next to an enormous column. Wearing headphones. Later, that's how I remembered seeing her. Just then, Katya and Nadya jumped off another train, tons of stuff in their arms: backpacks, bags, parcels. We left the station. Kropotkinskaya station – named in honour of the anarchist Peter Kropotkin.

We waited in a café for the latecomers. For some reason, we drank ice-cold Cola. For an hour and a half.

let's go

The time came. The church was 200 metres away. Or 300. Me in my Cossack hat, the girls in Orthodox headscarves – we walked towards the church as if we were floating. The entrance loomed up ahead.

> *'To secure unhindered entry into the place of worship,*
> *the accused wore clothes fully in keeping with the*
> *requirements of such places of worship; thus, under the*
> *guise of ordinary visitors, they entered the church.'*

An empty square in front of the church. There are no beggars. I don't think the beggars were against sitting there, but the propriety of the church wouldn't allow them.

church for the wealthy

Amid the clicks of cameras, tourists taking photos, we approached the iron gates of the metal detector.

'Put your backpacks on the table and open them, girls.' The morning faces of the guards are fatigued and lazy. I open my backpack.

One by one.

How do you smuggle an electric guitar into a secured tourist site? We had tried out various methods over the course of the previous month. First, the guards had demanded that I leave the guitar – in the case or out – under the window by the entrance. Then we decided to try out an enormous hiking backpack and a man who spoke perfect English, smuggling the guitar inside the church with the help of both.

'Knives?'
'No.'
'Proceed.'

everything, but the knives

I close my backpack without glancing up and go in. The main thing is that they don't find the guitar. Petya had the guitar.

'Young man! Wait a moment.'

In our plan, Petya was the foreigner, the man who spoke perfect English.

'What's in your backpack?'
'Nothing special,' he answered in English.

Usually, Russian security guards get completely flustered by charming foreigners. It worked. The amp was also in that backpack.

nothing special

We left the cold weather outside the church. It was 11 a.m. The cathedral was nearly empty, except for people in green uniforms tending the devotional candles.

'We have to act like ordinary girls in church.'

What do ordinary girls do in church?
'No idea.'

We decided to go up to one of the women tending the candles and ask where it would be best to light one.

'Where can we place our candles?'

While she explained the procedure for lighting our candles, which we didn't in fact have, I looked behind her and saw the low barrier surrounding the altar and the green carpet leading towards the altar gates.

The carpet is the same colour as her uniform, I thought.

'Thank you,' Nadya said.

green carpet to the altar

We walked around the edge of the church and reached a corner. The guards seemed alarmed. There was no time to lose.

We went up to the low barrier guarding the altar. Katya was the first to hop over. Because she's Katya. She just hops over and she's off. Nadya hopped after her, and then everyone else followed. I thought, I'm wearing this uncomfortable coat that weighs a ton, I'm going to get stuck on something, I'll fall and bring the whole barrier down – it's an accident waiting to happen. How am I going to jump around in this heavy thing? It is long, almost to my ankles. Why the hell did I wear this damn thing to an action? What was I thinking, – putting it on at a time like this?

And then I hopped over, too. I was the last one to jump, just as the candle-tender was running up to me looking a bit freaked out.

> *'The careful planning and coordinated actions of the performance allowed the group to carry out their criminal intentions in their entirety.'*

We needed to plug the guitar into the amp. Katya was responsible for that, for the guitar. She threw off her outer clothing and started taking the guitar out of the case. The security guards considered this to be particularly non-Orthodox.

the guitar is an un-orthodox instrument

> *'Ms Samutsevich, carrying out her criminal role, with the knowledge and assent of all the participants, took out an electric guitar.'*

The security guards grabbed Katya. She managed to distract them all, and this bought us 40 seconds to do our performance. 40 seconds of crime.

40 seconds

> *'what was the music like?'*
> *'goodness me, I don't know how to describe it'*

> *'was it church music?'*
> *'no, certainly not!'*
> *'you mean to say it was not church music?'*
> *'absolutely not'*
> *'what did the instrument sound like?'*
> *'I don't know what to compare it to, but it wasn't at all
> Orthodox'*
> *'what are Orthodox sounds?*
> *'I can't answer that!'*

> *judge: 'you are obliged to answer the question'*

We scramble up the stairs towards the altar, dropping our backpacks by the Holy Gates. They symbolize the gates to heaven. Women are only allowed to stand on the green walkway before the gates – the soleas – if they are cleaning women. Or brides. In Russia, there are no women priests. In Russia, there is Pussy Riot.

We shed our clothes. The outer layers.

We put on our balaclavas.

> *'Alyokhina was wearing a blue mask. She wore a dress
> that was somewhere between pink and red, green tights,
> and a bra that was falling from her shoulders.'*

I remember: I open my mouth to sing and everything around me – the whole church – seems to freeze. It is motionless. The sound dies away. There is only the echo of our uncoordinated screaming and shouting. Too many eyes on the icons.

time stood still

The security guards try to catch us.

> *'Alyokhina's dress was longer than the others', and she*
> *had to kick her legs higher.'*

It looked like some bizarre folk dance: he runs up to you, you run backwards; he runs again, you run in a different direction.

> *'Voice answered voice; word answered word,'*
> *the candle-tender said during the trial.*

Almost a compliment.

It was the most absurd prayer.

> *'We tried to get them off the ambo. They wouldn't leave,*
> *they resisted and ran back up again, then fell to their*
> *knees and started crossing themselves. This was*
> *humiliating and offensive to me.'*

Two men take my hands and lead me to the exit. The balaclava slips sideways and restricts my breathing. It's unclear who is leading whom. The church is still frozen, until one small figure, an old woman, starts to move. She screams, 'Girls! Girls! What are you doing? You're ruining yourselves!' We kept walking, and I thought, What, am I now ruining myself?

They took us to the exit and let us go.

We stood there, looking at the street.

Not a single police car. Katya was waiting for us by the entrance.

We started to run. And I thought, Where are we running to?

Why are we running, if there's no one after us?

Who are we running from?

Why can't we just walk to wherever we're going?

The security guards stayed on the job. There were no cops in sight.

why are we running?

Why are we running, then?

3. Operation 'Escape'

riot mama

Right after our 'Punk Prayer' performance, I took the metro to my son's kindergarten – it was noon.

I rushed inside, flying past the security guard. Green tights, raspberry-coloured dress. The balaclava sticking out of my pocket.

'Goodness, you look like you're going to a party!' the teacher said.
'Really?' I answered. 'I didn't notice.'
'Very pretty dress!' the teacher said. 'And Phillip has just woken up from his nap.'

15 days, at the most!

It was still light outside when I arrived at our conspiratorial headquarters. The editing of the 'Punk Prayer' video was in full swing. There was an argument about whether we should post it online – the quality of our performance did not inspire confidence. After all, we'd only managed to sing a single verse. The future of our group was also at stake. The Kolokol security guards had confiscated our guitar and given it to the police.

'What are we going to do without a guitar?' Katya said. 'We have to go to the police and get it back. They'll throw us in jail for 15 days, tops. I can live with that, no big deal.'
'Are you crazy?' Nadya said. 'Go to the *police*?'
'Sure. Fifteen days, at the most!'

We decided to post the video first and worry about the guitar later.

We never saw the guitar again.

an attack at dawn? i won't complain

The next day I took Phillip home from kindergarten and we discussed dinner. Phillip wanted ice cream first and I objected. We started to argue as we got into the elevator. When the doors opened, I saw two men in leather jackets standing on the stairs, right outside our door.

'You'll have to come with us.'
'Who are you?'
'Police.' They held up their badges in my face.
'What's happened?'
'Yesterday some chicks were dancing in church.'

chicks dancing in church

The action in Red Square; the police station; my ID with my address; the raspberry-coloured dress – the events of the past month formed a chain, and this chain led right into my closet. The raspberry-coloured dress was hanging there.

What to do? I couldn't remember anything from the manuals on how to behave when you're being arrested. I couldn't remember because I'd never read any of them. But they were all over the web. That thought stuck in my head like '?' can on a keyboard.

unfamiliar with the manual

'What chicks? What church?' I said. 'I know nothing about it. I have a small child and ice cream melting all over the place.'

I'd bought two minutes. I ran into the apartment and screamed into the phone at Nadya, 'They've come to arrest me. We have to do something. We *probably* need to find a lawyer.' After giving Phillip his ice cream, I returned to the front door.

rule #1: find a lawyer

'Write that you'll come tomorrow, and sign it.'
'Do I have to?'
'Sign!'

I signed a paper saying I would come to see them the next day. I gave it to a grumpy dude with a cheap-ass phone.

We immediately had a Pussy Riot meeting in a café. We decided not to go to the police and to stick together.

In the morning, Phillip watched cartoons. 'I'll be back soon,' I said. I collected my bag. He was four years old. In three months, he would turn five. 'I'll be back soon,' I said again, and locked the door. I came back two years later.

rule #2: after making a call, remove the sim card, and change your location

'After you make a call, remove the SIM card and go to another metro station. This is for your safety,' the lawyer said, and left to go to the police station in my place to find out what was going on.

That day, 23 February, central Moscow was almost empty. There were police everywhere downtown. People in camouflage uniforms were spread out in the side streets, hanging around the terraces of all the cafés. I had already taken apart my phone and put it back together again a hundred times. I was meeting the lawyer in ten minutes, and I was convinced I'd found the perfect hiding place – a café bathroom. I didn't want to come out. The whole place was crawling with people in epaulettes and camouflage.

'And the Leader said to his regiments,
"Men, is Moscow not with us?"'

khaki-skin

I could hear the television blaring inside the café: a live broadcast. Putin is at the stadium, surrounded by a huge crowd, reading a poem by Lermontov. It's on every channel.

> *Let's die near Moscow,*
> *As our brothers died.*
> *And we vowed to perish*

And we kept our vow of faith
In the Battle of Borodino.

The Battle of Borodino? I thought. Is he in his right mind? All the traffic in Moscow is shut down and the city is swarming with police because Putin decided to call out a bunch of supporters-for-hire and recite poems to them? And this had to happen now, of all times, when the police are looking for me. 'It's my lucky day,' I muttered under my breath as I walked along Kamergerskiy Lane to meet the lawyer, and bumped into one of the uniformed men. He appeared out of nowhere, on the pavement, flooded in sunlight. Behind him were two more; they all wore light blue berets. A thought went through my head: Strange, NKVD officials used to wear those, too.

'Oh, excuse me,' I managed to say.

Before we even said hello, the lawyer told me, 'Don't go to the police. They've issued a warrant for your arrest. Run.'

run, masha

We went into hiding somewhere on the outskirts of town, where the city turns into countryside. We switched off our phones as soon as the train came into the station. We hurried, certain that we were being tailed, constantly turning around, then separating to reach the apartment we were going to hide in by different routes. We stayed in that apartment for several days.

rule #3: use cash

'We have an interview scheduled with Al Jazeera.'
'But we don't have a single balaclava left.'

'So what? We'll go to the store and buy hats, then cut them up. We've still got two hours before the interview, there's plenty of time.'

'What if there's not enough time to get them?'

'We'll wrap ourselves in sheets.'

'We can't do that! It's Al Jazeera. They'll think we're terrorists!'

We found some hats in the only second-hand shop around. We stood by a wall trying to set up Skype on an old laptop so that our four heads fit on to one screen. We kept interrupting each other in the interview, saying that we didn't want to harm anyone or cause any trouble, that criticism and protest are not a crime, that our performance was not blasphemy but criticism of the institution of the Church and contemporary Russia. Who were we trying to convince? Who?

rule #4: don't show up in the obvious places

It was the season of Maslenitsa. The devil's holiday. Carnival. Maslenitsa is the week when the winter dies. Saying goodbye to winter in Russia means burning effigies, dressing up in costumes, eating pancakes, sledging down icy slopes.

We didn't have an effigy to burn. But next to our apartment was a wonderful hill of snow. We found a few cardboard boxes on the nearest rubbish dump. Tearing them into pieces to make sleds, we went down the hill again and again until we were completely covered with snow. When we'd run from our homes, none of us had thought to take extra clothes. We were all wearing whatever we'd been able to grab. I, for example, was wearing someone's (wonderful) old sailor shirt.

amateur revolutionaries

'Hey, we look like witches!' I shouted, trying to keep up with the others on our way back to the apartment.

'We *are* witches!' Nadya shouted back.

In the evening, we made pancakes and ate them. We didn't know that this would be our last Maslenitsa celebration for a few years. We stayed up half the night, talking and laughing.

forgiveness sunday

We were woken by an early-morning phone call. Someone pressed the loudspeaker button.

'Did you hear?'

'Hear what?'

'Turn on the news. They're going to prosecute.'

Silence.

don't watch the news

We were charged with 'Disorderly conduct, committed with the purpose of inciting religious hatred by a group of persons in an intentional conspiracy', according to Article 213, Section 2, Subsection (b) of the Criminal Code of the Russian Federation.

It's 24 February, Forgiveness Sunday. The significance of the day is enshrined in these words: 'If you forgive others their sins, our Father in Heaven will forgive yours, and if you do not forgive others their sins, our Father will not forgive yours.'

We left the flat in a hurry.

rule #5: don't go online from home

After the performance in the church, everybody wanted to interview us. We gave our interviews via Skype. We weren't supposed to go online at the places where we were staying. Where we spent the night, more accurately. We changed apartments every few nights. We tried our best to keep hidden.

bread with kefir

We had no money to eat at cafés. We had no money at all. We ate bread and buttermilk, and tried to go online using random free Wi-Fi hotspots. I'd brought a small camping stove and a canister of gas from home. We used it to boil water and make coffee. We had to give interviews in our balaclavas. 'Millions of viewers at home' were unfamiliar with our faces, and we planned to keep it that way.

girl with a camping stove

Giving an interview over Skype while wearing a balaclava and sitting in a café without ordering anything is weirder than ordinarily sitting in a café without ordering anything. So, we hid in the toilets. All three of us would go in together, lock the door for half an hour, and hold three interviews. Then we would move to another café. After a while, the employees naturally became alarmed and would start knocking on the door. What must those poor people have thought? Some woman had locked the bathroom door from the inside and was shouting in broken English about Putin's third term. They would turn out the lights and bang on the door.

Once, one of us left a balaclava in the stall. The waitress brought it back to us.

the talented conspirators

We had no money for the metro either, and someone who had promised us shelter for the night suddenly changed his mind. We ended up in the apartment of a bohemian theatre director who lived nearby. The place was being renovated, and the room we were given was stuffed with various sofas. We drank red wine.

'Which two books would you take if you had to be away from home for an indefinite period of time? Which do you think I would take?' a friend asked.
'Not the Bible, I hope.'
'Mandelstam and Rilke. You can always find a Bible.'

you can always find a bible

In the morning, I woke early because it was hard to breathe. The windows were blocked by sofas. Everyone else was still sleeping. I went to church. I couldn't believe our action had inspired hatred. I asked for a priest. The priest was eating lunch. I sat on a bench inside and waited. It was an old, dilapidated church. The priest came out after his meal.

I said, 'Do you know about the dancing in the church?'
'I heard about it.'
'Did you know that those girls might end up in jail, that they're being charged with a crime?'
'Well, they deserve it.'

He couldn't have cared less. He was still chewing on his lunch. I was wearing the same coat and the Cossack hat I'd worn in the Cathedral of Christ the Saviour. I had truly pinned my hopes on this priest. I believed that he would look at me and say something completely different. But we'd been charged for political reasons, and the priest agreed with the charges. He agreed with the TV.

I left the church. I sat on the steps and looked at the sky. There was no sun.

rule #6: change your appearance

In the photographs posted by the police, I had my hair down. It occurred to me that if I hid my hair under a hat when I went outside, no one would recognize me. So I stuffed it under a hat. A white, knitted cap. Wearing tinted glasses in winter would have been too suspicious, so I started wearing regular glasses. I thought that hair up + hat + glasses = an unrecognizable Masha. I changed my coat, too. My grandmother's Cossack-officer coat was too conspicuous. I borrowed a black one from the Bass Player. Someone else's black coat.

hair up + hat + glasses =

That night, we went to the Bass Player's and talked until morning. Until sunrise.

This was where we had recorded the Pussy Riot songs. The Bass Player sang the whole 'Punk Prayer'. It's her voice you can hear in the video; the whole world heard it. This was the apartment we left to go to rehearsals. We had ridden the same metro train and been late together. It was less than two weeks ago. I looked at her and couldn't believe it.

two heroines

Maybe if I hadn't asked the Bass Player questions the night before our action, she would have come, too. Which would mean that now, this morning, she would be leaving her apartment with us. There is a moment when two heroines of the stage understand that their fates will now unfold in different directions.

She said, 'You probably want to sleep now.' And she made up a bed on the sofa in the kitchen. The cheapest kind of a Ikea sofa, with black upholstery.

The next day, the police came to the Bass Player's; but we were already gone.

1984

The police were after us.

Now there were five of us in a small car, driving through night-time Moscow. In that moment, Moscow was no longer the familiar city with apartments and cafés where we had all met. Now, it was a map with bright points of light shining on the road up ahead – the traffic police. We only saw these points of light. On the one hand, we needed to pass them slowly, no speeding up at all; on the other, we wanted to fly by at maximum speed – every one of these posts could have meant our last taste of freedom.

wear a disguise

We got out of the car on the outskirts of the city, in a distant residential area.

We went up the stairs of the building and rang the doorbell. A grey-haired man of average height opened the door. He smiled.

'Do you know who this is?' Petya, our Englishman, asked me.
'No.'
'You should. This is Podrabinek.'

We proceeded into a small kitchen, where the table was set, and started to talk. Alexander is a dissident, author of a book called *Punitive Medicine*. It is an indictment of the Soviet authorities, who sent people who disagreed with them to psychiatric hospitals. They diagnosed people with 'mild schizo-phrenia'. Before Podrabinek was sent into internal exile in Siberia, in 1978, for 'slandering the Soviet system', the security services offered him the opportunity to leave the country. He refused and was sentenced to jail in 1980 for continuing to write about punitive psychiatry.

'When did you get out?' I asked.
'In 1984,' said Podrabinek.

We read copies of the *Chronicle of Current Events* until mid-night. It was a magazine that had been put out by Soviet dissidents, for which they had been given unbelievably long terms in the colonies and internal exile. We joked that, if they caught us, we would be the new dissidents. Which was just what happened.

Podrabinek was the first person in all that time to say, 'You should be proud of what you did.'

you should be proud

On our last day, we moved from one café to another in down-town Moscow.

'We have an interview in an hour,' Nadya said, settling down with a huge backpack on a bench in Starbucks.
'Okay. I'm going to go for a walk,' I said, and went outside.

the last day

It's very unsettling, knowing they could grab you at any second. That any random passer-by could turn out to be an undercover agent. I looked at people's shoes. Agents wear shoes with pointy toes. That's their idea of fashion. They also wear money belts. I went towards the metro. Two autozak police vans were wait-ing by the entrance. I went into a church.

autozak by the church

While I was standing in the church, I felt as if the other people there were about to surround me, drag me by the arms into one of the autozaks, and that no one in the world would know about it. No one. The priest was reading the liturgy. In prison, every night for several months I would dream about how we were on the run.

every night in my dreams I ran

Every night in my dreams I ran – and I still woke up in prison.

and every night I woke up in prison

When I left the church, the autozaks were gone.

'Where were you?'
'In church.'
'What?'
'Never mind.'

We locked ourselves in the bathroom at Starbucks and gave an interview via Skype for half an hour. The waiters turned off the light, tugged at the door handle, and threatened to call the manager. I wanted to shout, *What do you mean, the manager? There are a couple of police divisions looking for us in every corner of Moscow!* But we used our phones as improvised lights and just continued the interview.

it's our country

I can't say how long we thought we could keep running and how we thought it would all end. People offered to help us leave the country – we refused. There were various options: to go deep into Russia, far from the capital. Good people invited us to stay with them in secluded places. But that would be voluntary exile. Why would we agree to that? (No doubt some people would. Not us.) We didn't start this whole thing just to disappear.

we won't disappear

Revolution is a story. If we fell out of it, disappeared, it would be their story, not ours. Their country, not ours. We never took off our masks. We had never left the church. My T-shirt: 'To back down an inch is to give up a mile.' No sense in wearing those words if you don't live up to them.

Here was Putin running for a third term, and many people, in despair, left the country. But we didn't want to emigrate. In our story, personal choices are political.

they're the ones who should disappear

We spent our last night together in an enormous apartment.

'If we keep going to different cafés, they'll never find us,' Katya said. 'Also, how come there's no grechka?'

the last night

Meat patties, pasta, vegetables: everything ready for us to eat – but no grechka. 'There just isn't any,' Katya grumbled, and opened every cupboard in the kitchen, one by one. We started to laugh.

'What's so funny?' Katya asked.

Nadya and I climbed into the jacuzzi, lit every candle we could find. Night. A huge, empty sleeping apartment in the centre of Moscow, ours for just one night.

the royal night

'If we had got good grades, we could live in an apartment like this,' we said, trying to joke, and sinking into the hot water. We didn't feel like sleeping. I read:

> *I know in Hell I will be*
> *An artist of Hell-wide repute.*
> *They will seat me under a tree*
> *And issue me a gold flute.*

in hell i will be

In the morning, we left. With our backpacks. As we approached the metro, they descended on us right by the entrance. I never even saw their shoes.

About ten of them, all in black.

'Stop! Don't move!'

They surrounded us in a tight circle. Then we were staring at the high metal fence they had rammed us up against. We laughed. Well, that's it, girls. This is as far as we're going. No more running.

'What are you looking at? You'll never be able to jump over this.'

They were very smug.

rule #7: never give names

They shoved us into a car and wouldn't tell us where we were going. We didn't talk and didn't call each other by name. You shouldn't talk when cops are around. I tried to figure out what they were allowed to do to us and what they weren't. How I should behave. I knew nothing. Except that I was supposed to flush my SIM card down the toilet. So they wouldn't get the phone numbers of other members of Pussy Riot.

'Hand over the keys to your apartment!' an agent shouted at Katya. He was three times bigger than she was.
'What apartment?'

'Where you were living!'

'We don't live anywhere.'

'You don't have a home?'

'No, life's been kind of hard, you know . . .' Katya said calmly.

They are used to us being afraid of them. Don't be afraid.

rule #8: destroy your sim card

'We're going to see the investigator,' one of them said. I tried to find my phone in my pocket to call the lawyer. The agent noticed and took the phone away. He pulled out the battery in a matter of seconds, handed it back to me, and said, 'Now you can call.'

'We haven't slept in a week. Trying to fucking find *you*.' The agent leaned back against the seat wearily.

'What's that yellow scarf for?'

'Huh?'

'You know, that yellow scarf. What is it? Are you some kind of gang?'

'Sometimes a scarf is just a scarf.'

rule #9: say nothing without a lawyer

The chief investigator, Artyom Ranchenkov, was extremely nervous. Journalists crowded at the gate of the building where he intended to begin questioning us, which clearly unsettled him. He walked and kept repeating, 'This was just banal hooliganism, straightforward ordinary hooliganism.'

banal hooliganism

Later – much later – he took me to the questioning room.

'Well, let's begin. Were you in the cathedral on 21 February?'
he said.
'You have no right to begin the interrogation without my law-
yer,' I said.
'So you were in the cathedral on 21 February?'
'I need to use the toilet.'

Our lawyer arrived while I was flushing the SIM card with the
contact information of the other Pussy Riot members who had
been in the church down the loo.

The investigator said, 'You will be detained for forty-eight hours.
For the time being. The court will then decide whether you may
remain free during the trial.'

The lawyer and I went out into the stairwell. We sat together
on a windowsill and smoked. It was 4.30 in the morning.

48 hours

'Were you ever inside?' I asked him, referring to prison.
'Yep.'
'So, is it as frightening as they say it is?'
'Not really. Soon you'll see that the doors have a mind of their
own. They open and they close. They open and they close. Then
they're locked.'

He was joking. He was probably trying to get me to relax. You're
already on your way there, and that's that. It's happened; you
can't change it. Before the arrest, when we asked him for advice,
he said, 'Best eat your evidence.' Also joking.

I looked out the window. There were woods. White stars. And red sparks from a bonfire.

'Out you go. The convoy has arrived.'

And they took us to a holding cell. Petrovka Street.

i committed no crime, and so i declare a hunger strike

The first stop – a holding cell – in the temporary detention centre on Petrovka Street. They can't keep you there for more than a week. That explains why everything is disposable and why it's so filthy. Synthetic sheets that constantly give off static electricity. The shocks hurt. Especially when you're lying down, and I was lying down a lot, since we immediately went on hunger strike.

not more than a week

I wrote: 'I have been arrested illegally. I have committed no crime. Therefore, I am on hunger strike.' In prison, it's not enough simply to announce something. You have to declare it in writing.

The insomnia starts almost straight away when you're on hunger strike. The second night. You are awake and want to eat something. You lie there and stare at the ceiling. The windows are covered with iron eyelashes, like blinds. Black and very thick, so the light can't pierce through. A window through which you can never look.

black window

Bask in your glory, free Fatherland of ours,
Eternal union of fraternal peoples,
Popular wisdom granted by our forebears!
Bask in your glory, our country! We are proud of you!

Broad latitudes for dreams and for life,
The future years open up before us.
Our faith in our Native Land gives us strength.
So it was, so it is, and so it will always be.

standard procedure

Do you know what happens in the first hours in prison?
A search.

They take you out of the dark autozak in handcuffs and bring
you to a room. Two bright fluorescent lights hang from the
ceiling. The paint is peeling from the walls, and in the corner
there is a small cage. This is where they do the search. Two
women in uniform take away all your things: phone, watch,
books. These things are prohibited. Then they tell you to get
into the cage.

'Take off your clothes. All of them!'

get into the cage

I took off my skirt, which was patterned with loud blue checks,
my T-shirt, and my underwear. I stood there naked. In a cage.
On the cold stone floor.

'Now do ten squats.'

'Why?'
'So we can make sure you don't have anything hidden *there*.'

squats

I squatted. Ten times.

'Now bend over.'
'What?'
'Too many questions.'

Just imagine.

You think it's nice to stand naked in front of cops? I think anyone would have the same reaction in this situation. But once I gave an interview to someone who insisted that, for most people, it's no big deal. That people are not as sensitive to humiliation as I think. That once a person is in jail, nothing surprises you. Well, that's simply not true.

If you stop being surprised by such things, you'll be turning your backside to them and bending over for the rest of your life.

turn your backside and bend over for the rest of your life?

We have the right to refuse. This is our right, yours and mine. You can't know all the laws by heart, you don't know what will happen if you refuse. But you have to try.

I asked a lot of questions. They don't like questions. They answer: 'These are our orders.' You learn the particulars of those orders as you go along. You learn it on your own skin. The law can be bent, and the degree of flexibility is something you can only test in practice.

its flexibility depends on you

Every time you refuse, it causes an uproar. You wouldn't want to undress in front of them, would you? I didn't. Why should I? So we have to say no. And see what happens.

saying no

Half a year went by before I realized I could say no when the guards said 'Bend over.' A whole year passed before I could justify my 'no' by citing Russian law and forcing a gasp from each person at a search who told me to take off my underwear or to squat naked. But on that first morning of captivity, in the holding cell at Petrovka, shaking from cold and lack of sleep, wanting to fall asleep right there in the cage, in the same room with women dressed in uniforms with epaulettes, I didn't think that I could make a choice.

The memory of that morning stayed with me throughout my sentence.

4. Isolation

'You can't joke about national symbols. I'd take a good belt and whip them with it.'
– Leader of the Russian Communist Party on Pussy Riot's
'Punk Prayer'

The door opens, a guard says, 'Come out,' and handcuffs me. I can easily pull my hands through them, even when they are tightened all the way.

'Look who they've dragged in! You call this a criminal?' the guard grumbles as he leads me up a flight of stairs. We enter a small room.

arrest someone like you

A round-faced detective with hair like a ginger cat is sitting there, surrounded by smoke and wearing a white sweater.

'May I call you Masha?' he begins, leaning back in his chair.

The weak March sun is shining through the window.

There's a short pause. I'm tired. I remain silent. I sit and rest my head against the wall.

'You have a son, don't you, Masha? You want to be free? Here's the deal: you tell me the names of the other members of Pussy Riot, and there's a chance the court won't hold you in custody after tomorrow but place you under house arrest instead.'

initial offer

'May I have a cigarette?'
'Sure. Here, take as many as you like.' He smiles.

I light up and start to smoke. The first, best cigarette of the day. I grab a few more.

'I think I might need to sleep a bit,' I say finally. 'Tomorrow's going to be a long day. Call the guard, if you don't mind.'

> *There's not much hope that the trial will be called off.*
> *They'll go through with it. They're unlikely to give me*
> *seven years, but they could easily give me two or three.*
> *My son's birthday is coming up in two months. I hope he*
> *has a proper celebration.*
> – My diary, Petrovka, March 2012

presidential elections

I will be voting in handcuffs. It's 4 March. Downtown Moscow, temporary detention centre on Petrovka. A room with windows completely sealed by wooden boards, a dim lightbulb hanging from the ceiling. Two cellmates. One weeps; the other rocks back and forth silently in the corner, chain-smoking. She has smoked the last one from her pack and now she will take mine. On hunger strike, insomnia, lingering headache. In the middle of all this, the clatter of an iron key in the lock of the iron door, and someone roars: 'You want to vote?'

I jump up from the bed.

'So get going!'

Downstairs, there's a large room, elegantly appointed. A podium with wooden panelling, the national coat of arms, a large portrait of Putin.

'Where do we vote?'

A guard leads me to a small cubicle. I take a ballot, draw a large X across it, and write 'Russia will be free.'

russia will be free

'What's taking you so long in there?' the guard asks.

I walk out proudly, and we return to the cell. My stomach is cramping from hunger. Our toilet, a small hole in the floor on a raised platform, has a terrible stench. I can't rid my mind of the parallel between the podium in the hall and the podium in our cell with the stinking hole. Radio Russia drones on the whole day, talking about how Putin is winning from the Far East to central Russia. Someone pounds on a door with a fist, shouting, 'Turn that crap off!' But no one turns it off.

will someone turn that crap off?

The guard makes the rounds of four cells and examines us through the peephole. Now he looks even more often, as though my writing is putting my life in danger. He walks from cell to cell, bending down to look in each peephole. He works his shift every three days. So he has a one-in-three chance of developing scoliosis. He is either a brave man or he has read Victor Hugo, or, on the two days when he stays home, he makes sure to bend in the other direction.

the rounds

Every guard is being polite. They lead me down the short corridor twice a day, without tightening the iron bracelet, without shouting, 'Face the wall!' as they did on the first day, when I was more frightened than I am now.

8 March: International Women's Day. My fifth in prison. One Pussy Riot girl who took part in the 'Punk Prayer' but had not been captured by the police came to protest in front of the detention centre, wearing her balaclava.

Orthodox activists came to break up the protest.

Boris Nemtsov and Alexei Navalny, opposition politicians, also came. Exactly three years later, Nemtsov was murdered. By that time four criminal cases had been opened against Navalny.

38 petrovka street

Twice a day, they take me to see a nurse.

'Now, why did you girls have to go on a hunger strike?' she asks, leaning over me. (She is as cold as her stethoscope. She has red, permanent, chemical curls.) 'I read in the paper this morning that they were going to release you today.' And she smiles.

release!

'It's time you started eating again. Shall we?' she suggests, as kindly as she can, and asks her assistant for a thermometer. Epaulettes gleam beneath her white lab coat.

I say: 'Go to hell!'

go to hell!

I try to fall asleep. I close my eyes and see tempting slices of pizza floating in front of me, one after another. I know that there are some sweets in the cell, in a metal locker, and no one will see if I eat them. The thought of it is nearly driving me crazy. It's not chocolate, not a Snickers bar – just ordinary hard, sucking candy.

> *'Ah, these little hands aren't made for handcuffs,' one of the convoy escorts muttered sweetly, and fastened the iron cuffs until they left red stripes on my wrists.*

pizza

After some time, they bring in Old Nina, a wonderful person. She burnt her husband with an iron. Not to death, but severely. About eighty per cent of her speech consists of cursing. At night, she dreams about Stalin.

'Eh, Stalin would've dealt with you all.'

Later, she admitted to being a Jew. 'Just don't tell anybody,' Old Nina said.

red stripes

Nadya and I wait three hours before the first hearing. We sit in the basement, handcuffed to the bench. My legs are trembling from the effects of hunger. A group of coquettish convoy escorts surround us and offer some tea. Upstairs, a crowd of journalists and Orthodox activists mob our supporters.

> '*Some guys appeared out of nowhere, camouflage jackets, sneakers. They started moving towards me. One of them grabbed my placard and wouldn't let go. He punched me in the face, and I flew on to the asphalt. I realized that the whole protest was going to turn into a bloody mess. The police just stood there doing nothing. There were about fifty of them, and they didn't make a single arrest.*'
>
> – Taisiya Krugovykh, film director, *Pussy vs. Putin*

'What did you say to the journalists?' I asked Nadya.
'I said it didn't matter to me whether they convict us or not. The idea of an individual is a function of society.'

function of society

Nadya said something about social function while I sat there for three hours thinking, *Damn, my hair is a mess.* My hair *was* a mess and there was no comb or brush. It was so frustrating. How could I think about society if I had no way to brush my hair?

hair

'Forms of preventive punishment other than pre-trial
detention allow the suspect to disrupt the investigation,
to hide, to continue to engage in criminal activity.'
– The judge's order for custody, Taganky Court, 5 March

under arrest, for 2 months

On the way back to Petrovka, Nadya and I rode side by side in
an autozak for the last time. After that, under the investigator's
orders, they had to transport us in iron cages inside the autozak.
These were the height of an average person. The cages were
designed to prevent criminals from discussing the details of
their trial or planning new crimes.

of course we were planning to commit new crimes

SIZO No. 6, the only women's detention centre in Moscow, is
located on the outskirts of the city, in an industrial district. A
cruel-looking building made of yellow brick.

They unload us from the autozak; we're carrying some sad plastic bags. I haven't eaten in more than a week, and my legs start
to buckle under me. I have some idea of what I must look like
when I see Nadya, who has also not eaten in a week. A pale girl
with dark circles under eyes that are swollen with weariness.
Right away, she asks, 'Masha, what's up?'

sad plastic bags

They take us to the showers. Filth. Mildew on the walls. You
have to bring your own soap, and we don't have any. They give
us sheets. I roll up the pillow inside the mattress and grab them
with both arms. Then I walk down the corridor. After not

eating for so long, the mattress feels unbelievably heavy. I am out of breath after taking a few slow steps and after every fourth stair climbing the flight of stairs.

stairs, stairs

'My god, it's so high up,' I say to Nadya, who is bent over, lugging her own huge rolled-up mattress.
'I don't know how we're going to make it.'
'I don't, either. And this is just the beginning. We have to walk and walk.'

all the things

The first hunger strike is like first love – very confusing. Later, you get used to it; but the first time there is only pain, leg cramps, nightmares. Still, it's worth it. Otherwise, what will I tell you about?

quarantine

Nadya and I can't stay in the same room because we're partners in crime.

The mattress has blue and white stripes, like the colours of a police car. A long corridor, one flight of stairs, a second, a third and, finally, the door of my cell. It slams shut, and with a clank and a clatter it's locked behind me from outside.

striped mattress

'Boss, it's so cold in here! Please, give me a blanket!' my new neighbour shouts to the officer on duty. 'Boss, did you remember about the glasses? You promised!'

From behind the door, I hear the sound of steps fading away. Why do they speak to each another like this? I bend in weariness and throw the mattress on to the floor.

My only cellmate, Nina, and I sleep on the iron beds in our outdoor clothes. She wears a fur coat, and I wear an overcoat. It's so cold in the cell that we walk around with red noses and frozen toes. You aren't allowed to get into bed and under the covers until lights out. The gaps in the windows are plugged with sanitary pads and breadcrumbs. At night, the sky glows orange from the streetlights.

orange sky

I wrote that I had gone off the hunger strike; now I drink dark-coloured water (tea) with bread crusts three times a day. The iron bedside tables are so terrifying, they look like they could kill you if you banged your head on one of the corners.

coloured water

I'm still not able to sleep. Today they threatened me with solitary confinement for not folding my blanket properly.

solitary confinement

Nina keeps saying it can't get any worse. Nina doesn't believe in change. Today is the first day that I can walk normally. I exercised for twenty minutes in a small square with concrete walls and a rusty grille overhead.

run, masha

In SIZO No. 6, you aren't allowed to receive any books
except the Bible. They accepted one today from my
mother at the parcel reception point, but they still
haven't given it to me.

out of the bible

Nina is probably right, it won't get any worse than this.
It's bitterly cold. There are huge cracks between the walls and
the windows. Thousands of dried-up balls of dough. You don't
notice them at first. Then you realize what they are. You realize
what they are, but you don't understand what these thousands
of balls of dough are doing here. I can tell you: they're a way of
protecting yourself from the cold. Here and there, you can see
a sanitary pad. Cheap sanitary pads which they distribute to
the women here. They protect you from the cold, along with
the little balls of dough.

cheap sanitary pads and balls of dough

Fluorescent lights, those grim, dreary Soviet tubes. From 6 a.m. to
10 p.m., the light sears my eyes. I can't turn them off. At night, a
yellow lightbulb burns above the door. No one's allowed to use a
torch: electrical equipment is forbidden. Candles are forbidden.

access to light is forbidden

There is no logic to these 'laws'. I can have an immersion
coil, but not a kettle. What is an immersion coil? A dangerous
object, banned in most European countries. A burning immersion
coil can be used to kill. I can have a coil. But not a kettle.

no logic

A table connected to a shelf with iron bars. This 'bench-table' structure is bolted to the floor. Just in case I take it into my head to fuck someone up with it. Such garbage.

I want to fall and fall asleep. Fall deep into sleep.

I'm wrapped in a blanket, but my teeth still chatter from the cold.

'Rise and shine, ladies!' shouts the warden in a voice that used to be a woman's, and bangs on the iron door with an iron key.

don't obey

She looks through the peephole. My cellmate bounces up from the iron mesh of her bed like a ball. I remain where I am. The warden goes away and I think: she still has to wake up half the prison, it's 5.30 in the morning, I've got no energy at all.

'Which part of rise and shine do you not understand?' I hear when she next bangs on the door.

I can't fall asleep immediately after nine days of hunger strike. It's the first day since I started eating again. I only managed to sleep right before morning. Won't she just go away? Turning over on my side, I draw my legs up under my coat against the cold.

'You're only making it worse,' my cellmate says, shaking her head. 'They can turn really fierce sometimes.'

wrapped in a blanket

At this very moment, the door opens with a clang.

'You think this is a fucking holiday resort? Or are you deaf? Get out of bed now, scum!'
'Now, that was uncalled for,' I mumble through my sleep. 'Why, may I ask –'
'Think you're so smart, scum? I said, Get up!'

I drag myself up off the bed.

> *'Patriarch Kirill claimed that the country has no future if the mockery of sacred things becomes a form of political protest. He noted that it pained him to see how people who call themselves Orthodox Christians are defending Pussy Riot.'*
> – News item, 24 March 2012

mockery of sacred things

I have a good mattress compared to my cellmate's. She has to fold hers double and lie on top of it just to feel there's something between her body and the bed's iron mesh. That's how thin it is.

a mattress folded double

The food hatch opens and breakfast bowls appear. A rank mixture of cabbage, tendons and sinews of some sort. I am a vegetarian. I drink tea and eat bread instead. But the bread isn't quite bread. It's rations.

rations that aren't quite bread

Sticky, it's made of the lowest-grade flour. It tastes something like bread, but after eating it for a couple of days I am stricken with a catastrophe down below – terrible sharp pains in my gut. Aside from this bread ration and some strange substance they insist on calling porridge, there is nothing I can eat. Everything else contains meat. Or something that is supposed to look like meat. Bearing a slight resemblance to it.

a shadow of meat

Pussy Riot were called provocateurs and the 'Punk Prayer' a provocation. For the first days and weeks they expected new provocations from us. Only, this time, not in a church but in a detention centre. What were they afraid of? That we'd stand on the tables and shout, 'God is a lie!' That we'd kill them with the immersion coil?

new provocations

I think they feared we could incite the other prisoners to over-throw the guards, to overthrow Putin. They themselves were afraid of being overthrown.

why not?

They were afraid that others would behave the same way as us.

Everything that happens to me is captured on video.
The camera is either pinned to the guard's breast
pocket or it's in her palm. The camera is always pointed
in my direction.

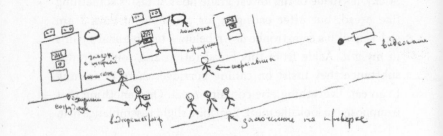

human rights advocates

A commission arrives: two human rights advocates. The guards at SIZO No. 6 are unhappy about this. Their video camera is visibly trembling in one of the guards' hands.

'Do you have any complaints?' one of the human rights advocates asks.

The guards standing in the back shake their heads, warning me not to complain about anything. They shake them from side to side.

Your heads are wobbling like Soviet toys, I almost say out loud.

soviet children's toys

'Do you have any complaints about being held in the detention centre?' one of the advocates asks, leaning over to me. She adds, 'You can tell me, I'm on your side.'

I look at her. At the grim, silent guards. At my cellmate. She is shivering from cold and tries to gesture to me to remind them she has poor eyesight.

'I suppose I have no complaints,' I say slowly.

The guards smile and nod in approval.

'But there are a few matters that are, to put it mildly, very puzzling,' I add quickly, nearly losing my composure. 'First, we haven't been sentenced yet. Guilt for the crimes we've been charged with has not yet been established. There are more than one thousand people being held here, and all of us are under investigation. We might still be proven innocent. Even if that doesn't happen, we're still human beings. Should human beings have to live in ice-cold rooms, stuffing bread crumbs into cracks in the wall to keep out the draughts? I don't think so.'

The human rights advocates go over to the windows and see that they are indeed plugged with balls of dough.

staying human

'The temperature in the room is within standard norms,' hisses the head doctor, who has joined the visitors.
'That is sacrilege, using bread for that purpose!' a guard shouts from behind the doctor.
'Why do you think we're wearing all our clothes? So we can stay warm, or maybe you think we want to be pretty when you film us?'
'So you want to joke around, do you?' the guard yells.

cold, cold, cold

'Second,' I go on seriously, 'the mattresses. At night, we sleep in our overcoats because of the cold, on mattresses that consist of nothing but rags. They've literally been disembowelled. My cellmate folds her mattress in two at night and sleeps on a portion about a foot and a half wide. And this morning, we woke up to shouting and cursing –'

'That's enough!' the guards shout, nearly in chorus.

no, it's not

The human rights advocates tell us they understand. They ask Nina whether she has any complaints. She answers in a barely audible voice, 'I need glasses. Honest to god, I can't see a thing without them. And the investigator took away the ones I had.'

'They should return her glasses,' one of the advocates says softly, turning to the doctor.

The doctor nods in silence.

The next day, without saying a word, they give us new mattresses.

And the day after that, my cellmate gets her glasses back. She has to sign a document to get them. The doctor notes that this has never been allowed to anyone before.

There's something to this, I think. I'll have to find out more about human rights advocacy.

fight!

Society as a notion doesn't exist in Russia. No one believes that there are things in the world that depend on them. On the contrary, everyone thinks that nothing depends on them.

I spent a week in quarantine, and I had the whole day, every day, free. If you call that freedom.

freedom within your cell

The time drags. Days become unbearably long.

I read the prison code. I brewed tea, drank it from an aluminium mug, a free aluminium mug. I later realize: you only get those mugs in a prison in the capital, you don't get them in other prisons. I walk around the cell. I write a letter. I don't have any envelopes. But you can write it now and send it later. Which is what I did.

A low brick square divided into compartments, miniature exercise yards. Rough, cold, black concrete covers the walls. A door leads into the square; then there are doors to each exercise yard that open off a long corridor of streetlights, just like a boulevard, a regular street, just as if they might open to the courtyard of a regular apartment block or a house. A sewage grate. I am a prisoner, and I'm going for a stroll. The light in the security camera blinks. My hands are behind my back. My hands are holding one another. The guard walks behind me. He tells me where to stop. The door closes behind me for an hour. I am a prisoner. I walk in a circle, crouch, stretch my arms out in front and crouch on a wooden bench. I stare at the gap between the mesh ceiling and the roof above it, stare right at the sky. The rain drips down, and the drops, like beetles, gouge holes in the cement, burrow canals between the holes, then live a communal life, in puddles. I make another round, then, after a running start, jump and plant both feet on

*the wall. Colourless chunks crumble off and sink into the
wetness. The ceiling above each exercise yard is a rusty
mesh of bars and lattice. Thick upright poles, rough-
hewn reinforcement. A guard oversees each exercise yard,
either moving around or standing still. Now he's
watching me.*

he's watching me

You count your last cigarettes. You realize no one on the outside knows that you are running out. In fact, no one knows that
you're now in this detention centre. That you've moved from
the old one. I have a pack and a half left. I smoke a pack a day,
and I don't know when they'll bring me more.

Finally, the lawyer arrives. I ask, 'What's the news?'

'Archpriest Chaplin is planning to visit Pussy Riot in
detention.'

'Is he bringing cigarettes?' I ask.

But Chaplin didn't bring me cigarettes. He didn't come to the
detention centre at all.

40 women

From quarantine, I was taken to the general cell.

40 women stream out all at once and surround me. On television the evening before – and they do have television – there
was a programme about us. It painted us as blasphemers, how
we danced in church.

'Why? Why did you do that?'
'Why?'

They are insistent; they demand to know.

Yesterday, they saw a person on TV and now they see the same person in the flesh. They had been forewarned: the ultimate talk show. The cell monitor had told them that a 'celebrity' was coming. They were waiting.

'What does "Pussy Riot" mean in Russian?'
'Pussy Riot is something like "Kitty Revolt". Then I add that, in English, the word 'pussy' also has another meaning. They say, 'Oh, so it's like "Cunt Revolt".' We all laugh and go into the kitchen. The most popular food here is Chinese instant noodles: *Doshirak*. They share some with me, too.

cunt revolt

There was nothing malicious in their questions, just bewilderment. When you talk to people, they change their opinion about you. People without cotton wads in their ears can change their minds quickly.

without cotton wads

The guards check us twice a day: first thing in the morning and right before bedtime. The cell door opens. Girls move out of the cell, one by one, hands behind their back, line up against the wall. The cell supervisor reports: 'Forty people in cell 203.'

'All good?' the inspector asks.
'All good,' the cell monitor answers.

'All good' is the only acceptable report. It must be 'all good', twice a day.

all good

. . . the girls gave me a nightgown with roses on it. It's sweet and white, and I look like a peasant. Through the window, you can see that the snow has almost all melted. In the morning, it smells like the sea here; in the evening, we don't open the windows. We have a lot of shoes; they stand in a row and make friends, though they have the potential to stomp on a cellmate's toe – I can see that clearly from up here. I sort of don't like it that the shoes aren't able to see the streetlights and that they are denied justice; but possibly the streetlight has faith in god, and the one divine invisible sandal touches its bright glow.

denied justice

'At tomorrow's inspection in the corridor, we go naked,' the cell monitor says.

In my hand, I hold a clear plastic bag with my belongings in it. This is all I have. After a few weeks in prison, I have come to understand how easy it is to fit life into a plastic bag, but after hearing the words of the cell monitor I drop the bag.

'What do you mean, naked?'
'Just that. You take everything off, wrap yourself in a sheet and step out of the cell.'
'But why?'
'Because tomorrow is Thursday.'

Naked Thursday is the dark secret of SIZO No. 6. At the evening inspection on Thursdays, the women line up wrapped in white sheets. When the guard and the prison doctor walk down the formation, they stop by each woman, who then unwraps the sheet and shows herself to them.

naked thursday

'But why?'

They say, 'We have to make sure the prisoners have no tattoos.'

What did we reply?
Nothing.
We unwrapped our sheets. One by one.

political

> *'The Minister of Foreign Affairs of the Russian*
> *Federation, Sergei Lavrov, called Pussy Riot's "Punk*
> *Prayer" "a blasphemy, a sacrilege". Some, he said,*
> *"including in the West, have in fact interpreted it as a*
> *freedom of speech, albeit frolicsome". But Russian society*
> *would not accept such behaviour.'*
>
> – News item, 20 March 2012

Officially, there are no political prisoners in the Russian criminal justice system. But, in official quarters, they called me a 'political' – a political prisoner, that is.

In prison, there's a lot you can do if you have money. I don't have money. It wouldn't matter if I did. If there's a clandestine phone making the rounds in the cell block, I don't know about it because I'm a political. With a political, regulations must be strictly enforced: no phones, no TV after lights out. Obey the rules.

The Bass Player sent me some books, they were taken down to the basement for inspection. Now I have to go and explain why Georges Sand and Simone de Beauvoir represent no sort of danger to anyone.

the danger of simone

After a few days, the prosecutor, a portly man, arrives. All the women stand in a line in front of him. He asks, 'Is everything in order?' And they answer, 'Everything's in order.' Then he takes me behind the iron door, and asks, 'Is everything satisfactory?' I remember he wore glasses. I tell him that, on Thursdays, the women have to stand in the corridor naked. He seems taken aback; his expression changes.

the prosecutor

Then he asks, 'Any other problems?'
'Books,' I say.

That is, the absence of them.

The library is a cardboard box full of romance novels under the bed.

It sounds like the only things I don't like are Naked Thursdays and romance novels.

I don't like naked thursdays and romance novels

After the prosecutor left, they moved me to another room. Fifteen minutes later. I had to roll up the mattress again. I was taken to a cell for people requiring closer supervision. A cell for four. No. 210. For people suspected of serious economic crime; ex-members of the police force; stool pigeons; people of my ilk.

I spent half a year in cell no. 210.

> *Today, Tarkovsky's* Nostalgia *is on TV. My cellmates are nice. Aya is nearly forty, but she's more like a child than I am. Larisa is truly bold and fearless, and she has a furry black cat curled up on her lap. The convoy escort is puffing and panting outside the window – they're bringing someone back from court. After midnight. Our 'Punk Prayer' is the subject of constant debate – good practice for making public statements.*

When someone gives a prisoner a pen and a piece of paper, the first thing she does is draws a calendar. Time doesn't exist in prison without a calendar.

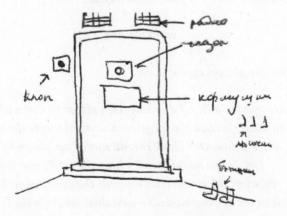

The first book I read in detention that came to me from outside was *And the Wind Returns*, by Vladimir Bukovsky.

The first book that robbed me of two days' sleep, because I read it cover to cover, several times, was *Kolyma Tales*, by Varlam Shalamov.

enemies of the state

Both books were written by Russian prisoners, so-called enemies of the state. Less than a year later, I would find myself in a penal colony near the one in the books: in the Perm region, in the northern Urals.

Shalamov was declared a 'socially dangerous element' and sent to a colony in the Urals almost a hundred years ago. At that time, in 1929, he had already clearly grasped why the government took these kinds of measures. He wrote: 'From the first moments in prison, it was clear to me that there was no mistake in the arrest, that it was the systematic destruction of a whole "social" group – all those who remembered what they were not supposed to remember from the past, from Russian history.'

wind returns

A story can always repeat itself.

Snowflakes fall. All day long, they either lie down like a starched sheet on the icy ground or whirl inside through the window. Our black cat, all puffed up, sleeps by my feet. In the background, I hear the kettle boil, water pouring; the steam rises towards the snowflakes. They melt in the air, warmed up – and then they're gone. For a

*few days, it seemed that nothing was left – nothing
existed any more at all. Only the metal rungs under my
back, and the changing light.*

changing light

The peephole in the door, the bugs in the visitors' room,
the snitch in the next bunk, and the searches, searches,
searches. Going to sleep on command, getting up on command, eating on command. Wait! Hands behind your back!
Face to the wall!

life-thought schedule

You have a routine; you have a set schedule for life and living.
Do you also have a set schedule for thinking? Why don't you
tell them no? Why can't you even think about telling them no?
Why does this thought seem pointless to you? When did it
become pointless for you?

snowflakes fall

They led me to an interrogation without handcuffs, but I had
to hold my hands behind my back. More than a year passed in
prison before I stopped holding my hands behind my back. It's
against regulations. Out of the question. Stopping is a victory.
Not to turn my face to the wall, not to put my hands behind
my back, not to spread my buttocks at their command – these
are my great victories. And they *are* great. Like winning a chess
tournament, if you weren't locked up. Dinosaurs walk again on
the floor of the Caribbean Sea.

anything is possible

Spring came yesterday. Pigeons are cooing under our window. The sky is overcast now, but when there's sun the rays shining through the bars make patterns on the floor, and in the illuminated squares you can see bright orange spots on the scrubbed floorboards. We suddenly have so many oranges! A huge tubful, plus a bucket! And lots of pears, too. The iron cupboard nailed to the wall is groaning under the weight of a carton of apples, kiwis, cakes and piles of cheese.

oranges

'Well, I've got news for you. A third member of your band has been arrested now,' the police detective says.

Two weeks after our arrest, Katya was summoned to an interrogation and arrested on the spot, in the interview room.

our third

'And you made a special trip here just to tell me this?' I say. Weeks after. At the end of March.

The cheerful grin fades from his face and is replaced by a grim, glowering expression.

'The best thing for you to do now is to plead guilty,' he says.
'Guilty of what?' I say.
'Of the crime,' he says, frowning.
'I don't intend to do that.'
'Why?'
'Because I'm not guilty,' I say, smiling.

Sitting at the table, the detective leans toward me and says in a quiet voice, 'There's more.'
'What is it?'
'Recently, we paid a visit to your son's kindergarten. We had a talk with the teacher.'

interesting news

Pleased by the fact that I had stopped smiling, the detective looks at me expectantly. A piece of white paper lies on the table next to his folded hands; he's ready to receive my confession of guilt.

'I understand that it isn't easy to admit to committing a crime. Let's begin with a simple admission that you were present at the scene,' the detective continues, in an intentionally calm voice.

'We'll begin and end,' I answer, as softly as possible, 'with you pressing the red button.'

red button

In every interrogation room, there is a red emergency button. To call the guard at the end of the proceedings.

The days were like snow – they melted away. They stayed in my memory only as dates, as the sound of boots shuffling through the April slush. I was like the iron bars on the window that trapped our world inside and the wind, damp with drops of water, that lurked in the corners. All else had gone, faded – the bars in the air had nothing to hold on to or to hold back, but they held on anyway, and the air became heavy and grey, indistinguishable from storm clouds.

april shuffle

Ranchenkov, the chief investigator, walks around with a briefcase and looks like a schoolboy. We meet in the interrogation room.

He blushes when I bring up the corporate parties in the church, puts his black briefcase on the table and starts filling out forms.

One of his hobbies is trying to identify a true embodiment of Russia's national identity. Putin and his ideologues' favourite current project. While we're waiting for my lawyer, we chat animatedly. About Ancient Russia and present-day Russia, about politics.

grade-school patriotism

Two months later, he'd stopped mechanically repeating that it was nothing but 'banal hooliganism'. Once, he jumps up and starts flailing his legs around, as though imitating my movements in the church.

'Is it really proper to kick your legs around like that?' he rants.

A chief investigator in a suit. Wearing a shirt with cufflinks. Terrible cufflinks, I told him right away. Do not wear them. Cufflinks generally suck.

legs around like that

Once a week, we prisoners go to a room with a shower and filthy walls that they call the sauna, or *banya*. While walking us there, the guard always follows behind. It's forbidden for them to show their backs to us because we're dangerous. (This outing is called '*banya* day'.)

hello, ussr!

'I have a little story to tell,' Aya says, chuckling. 'I can tell you why the revolution didn't take off.'

As they were leading Aya back from the sauna, she ran into Nik-Nik, which is the Dadaesque name we gave to one of the staff in the prison. He was known for drinking all the time. Nik-Nik was pushing a box in front of him with his foot.

'Maybe we can help you with that?'
'It's okay, I'll manage.'
'What's in the box?'
'It's just a bunch of votes for Prokhorov's opposition party. They told me to throw them in the garbage.'

democracy in the garbage

Whatever comes from outside – they cut it. Cheese,
apples, cakes. They take out any matches. Don't send
bread – they give us their own detention centre bread.
We cut off the crusts on all sides and eat them. We wrap
the soft insides in newspaper and throw them away.
Every day, it's like we're burying the bread and we
prepare it for the funeral.

burying bread

When you have a question, you have to 'crush the
bedbug', that is, press an old black button. Then a red
light turns on outside the cell. When the guard walks
down the corridor, he sees the light, opens the food hatch,
and says, 'Whatchya want?'

crush the bedbug

The door is solid metal with dents in it. Made by
fists. The guard often 'doesn't see the light'. That's
how fights start, hearts stop, and women go into
premature labour.

the ten-mile route

'Hi, Masha,' the detective says.
'Hi, Igor,' I answer.

After half a year of regular meetings with the red-haired chief
of criminal investigations, we've become familiar.

'Check this out.' He pulls a phone from his pocket. 'I rode 10 miles.'

On the screen of his old smartphone, we look at the route from the building where his boss, Ranchenkov, works, to my prison, to which he travelled on his bicycle.

'Cool,' I answer.
'Plus, I'm dieting now,' he boasts.

spring afternoon

The spring afternoon is fairly hot, and I open the sixth volume of the legal case they've drawn up, which Igor has brought me so I can inform myself. I begin to read:

'The following passage from the song also bears a negative and mocking character: "Virgin Mary, Mother of God, be a feminist!, be a feminist!" insofar as uniting the image of the Holy Virgin with feminism, some elements of which directly contradict the Orthodox faith, and which the Russian Orthodox Church does not hold in high regard, is an affront to devout Christians.'

virgin mary, be a feminist!

Are they for real? I think. I raise my head to discuss the issue with Igor and notice that he is asleep. His head is resting on the wooden table, which looks like a school desk, with his arms wrapped around it. His phone is lying next to it. The screen still shows his 10-mile route.

I read on: 'The combination of the lexeme "shit", which has an obscene excremental-anal semantic aura, and the lexeme "holy", in the phrase "holy shit", along with the repetition of this line, significantly intensifies its effect.'

'Holy shit,' I say out loud.
'Something wrong?' the detective says, lifting his head from the desk. There is a trace of his sleeve imprinted on his right cheek.
'Never mind,' I answer.

The next moment, he realizes that something irreparable has happened.

I say: 'Don't worry. I didn't call anyone, and I didn't eat a single page of the criminal report.'

excremental-anal semantics

I'm making soup. So far I've done this only once. It's forbidden, you can get sent to solitary confinement if they catch you, and our cell is small – it's easy to see what we're doing through the peephole.

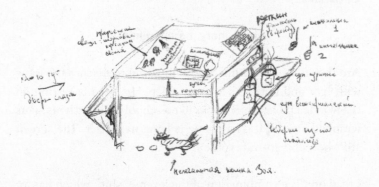

What is a criminal? Is it the people around me, myself included? 'From the moment of my arrest,' I write in my diary, 'so and so many days have passed.' I write this, but I don't believe a single word of it. I don't even believe the words 'the moment of my arrest'. I don't believe that 'arrest' is really 'arrest'; that a 'criminal' is really a 'criminal'. What is a criminal? A human being? And that's all?

The immersion coil is a dangerous object, but I've almost stopped being afraid of it. With the immersion coil, you can heat something up to boiling, but you can't boil something. I still cannot grasp the moment when something being heated transitions to being boiled. So, officially, I guess you could say we are heating vegetables in water, along with oil.

human criminal

They'll lock us up for a long time. It's as clear as day, this stuffy, empty day.

I walk around the ping-pong table in the five-square-meter stone box of a prison exercise yard. Only a strip of sky is visible – a grey strip between the iron mesh above my head and the concrete wall.

ping pong

I walk in circles with a book in a grey cover, two fingers planted in the middle, and repeat a verse of Mandelstam:

People who are hungry, who are sick,
Will kill, will suffer cold, will hunger.

And in his famous grave
The unknown soldier will be laid.

little grey book

It is still three years before the war between Russia and Ukraine and I have still not become an official enemy of the people; I retain my modest status of 'engaging in disorderly conduct'. It's still early days, as they say. But, later, they will say other things, and for the time being I'm walking around the tiny concrete exercise yard, my thirtieth round, and reciting more verses by heart . . .

blossoms

Our only kin is what is in excess.
Ahead lies no downfall, but a misstep,
And wrestling for sufficient air
Is not a glory that impresses others.

And overstocking consciousness
With half-waking routine living,
Do I have no choice but to drink this slop,
And eat my own head under fire in battle?

a few minutes

In a few minutes, the iron door to the exercise yard will open, and they will take me back to my cell. I will gather my papers there, and they will take me to a procedural meeting, to the chief investigator, to another building in the same detention centre, to a small office.

The investigator will tick boxes, bent over the desk like a school-boy. Next to him, proudly arrayed in fancy clothes, are the main plaintiff – the church candle-tender – and her lawyer.

get ready

'How's your cell? Spacious?' the plaintiff, a Christian, asks me.
'It's big enough,' I say, looking to the side at the window, from which the view is completely obscured by paint.
'How many of you are there?'
'Four, but we don't all spend all our time there, of course.'
'You mean they take you out for walks? How often?'
'Every day.'
'My, it sounds just like a health spa!'
'Want to trade places with me?'
'Masha!' Ranchenkov, the investigator, says. He started addressing me by my first name very early on.
'Yes,' I say.
'Let's start the procedure. Let's talk about the matter at hand. The case.'

the matter at hand

And we talk about the case. Everything is recorded officially, with signatures, serious expressions on our faces. The case is sizable; it fills seven fat volumes, sewn together with white thread. After sentencing, they will give me a copy, which I will take with me on the convoy to the penal colony in the Urals. There will be no exercise yards for walking there. The colony barracks are surrounded by open land, and in the summer (though it's against the rules) they let you grow flowers there. The soil is poor, so before planting the seeds it has to be weeded and watered repeatedly.

But the flowers grow and everyone is happy to look at a garden by the barracks. The guards no less than the prisoners.

a conversation on record

This May is hot and beautiful. The sky is swollen. Beneath it, black cars crawl along the broad streets like beetles. Their eyes are open and trained on the eyes of the Kremlin gates. Behind them, tanks crawl, and missile-carriers, like the hearses of iron corpses.

putin's inauguration

He says, 'We will get up off our knees and rise above the world.'

They say, 'Yes.'

6 may

Small old buses. Small old veterans holding red bunches of carnations in their dried-up hands. They weep. They are talking about them when they say: 'Victory'. And then drive them back to their apartments, where the ceiling is falling in.

victory parade

We look at the screen, our hands holding the window bars. The bars were forged five years ago, the floorboards conceal dust, the iron tables cannot be moved or removed.

they laugh while they sin

'Well, we won. We didn't plead guilty,' I say, as I'm leaving the investigator. He's standing in the doorway, his head drooping wearily, his arms hanging at his sides.

The case file is finalized and sent to the court.

'You didn't win,' he says. And, after a short pause, adds, 'You just didn't lose.'

5. Russian Trial

There are people who live their whole lives in constant fear, as though they are guilty of something. But if you are innocent, if you have not committed any crime, what is there to fear?

watch closely: they're changing history

A convoy escort with a dog leads the way, and we follow, entering the cage one by one. We extend our hands through a small opening. The convoy escort removes the handcuffs and hangs them on his belt. He sits on a chair by the cage. The dog sits next to him.

aquarium

Our cage in the courtroom is called 'the aquarium'. It's made of glass, and stands in the middle of the courtroom on the third floor. There is no microphone in the cage. You listen, and speak, through a narrow slit in the bulletproof glass.

'All rise! This court is in session!' a bailiff announces, and everyone stands up.

bulletproof

'The defendants pose a danger to society and might disrupt the judicial investigation. For this reason, they must be held in custody during the trial.'

The dog vomits at the entrance to the courtroom; the judge steps over the puddle.

> *'I am sickened by what they did, by their appearance, and
> by the hysteria surrounding everything that has happened.'*
> – Medvedev, former president, current prime minister

hysteria

'Masha, Masha! Get up!' says Aya, my cellmate and friend, yanking the sheet off me. I protest, and wrap myself tighter in the yellowing flannel rag, like a caterpillar.

'Masha, you'll sleep through the trial!' she shouts.

It's half past five in the morning.

5.30 a.m.

The mattress has to be rolled up and taken to another room. Prison regulations. So that if they release you, your mattress can be reassigned. But they won't release me.

I throw everything I might need into a bag. Dried fruit – prunes, apricots – walnuts for Katya; a fresh newspaper to read in the autozak; Deleuze's *Capitalism and Schizophrenia* for Nadya. Instant coffee in a clear plastic bag, cigarettes, carrot salad.

When you're leaving on a journey, you do the same thing. You try to fit your whole life into one backpack.

journey

I cut up some black tights to make laces for my sneakers. I put on a black dress.

They take me downstairs and put me next to Nadya in a cramped container in the basement – a glass and iron box resembling an elevator that doesn't go up or down. I smoke and read the newspaper: first about ourselves, then Putin, and then everything else. The smoke fills up the container so fast you nearly choke on it.

coffee and cigarettes

'Their only crime was being young, arrogant, and beautiful.'
– Patti Smith

'The punishment for their actions must be such that it would be terrifying to repeat them.'
– Sokologorskaya, the candle-tender and injured party

'You know,' I say to Nadya while we're sitting in the cage inside the autozak, 'everything that is happening to us is just unbelievable!'
'What, exactly?' asks Nadya, who prefers precise formulations.
'All of it. The whole thing!' I say, waving my arms around the smoky cage in excitement. 'The trial is like a show. If only we had a camera, we could film it, and it would be amazing!'

*'They are members of a band with a name that is very
unattractive in Russian: Pussy Riot.'*

– Pavlova, the injured party's attorney

motor

The autozak stops. The barred door opens. A woman convoy
escort in a blue uniform reaches her hand out to me, and I hold
my hand out to her. She claps on the handcuffs.

On the right, a fierce black Rottweiler is barking. On the left,
people call out, 'Be strong, girls!' The convoy escort is wearing
dangly earrings.

'Hurry up, move on through,' she whispers. 'What are you looking at over there?' And she leads me, handcuffed to her wrist,
to the building's basement. There are several holding rooms
there. She puts me in one of them, frisking me lightly. The door
closes with a gentle smack.

4, 3, 2, 1

'Get ready. You go up in five minutes!' the court guard shouts
from behind the iron door. 'Don't dawdle – no one's going to
wait for you.'

We walk through the deserted building, up three flights of
stairs, then along a corridor straight into the aquarium, the
bulletproof cage. This is where we will be prosecuted.

We hear the clicking of cameras. At first, the hundreds of clicks
seem to ring out like rifles.

shutter clicks

The courtroom is full of familiar faces. Friends I used to read poetry with, journalists I admire. Activists who joined us at demonstrations. My parents, who hadn't seen each other since their divorce, are sitting in the front row, faces frozen, revealing what looks like horror or some sort of strange rapture.

All the people I know stop being themselves and are transformed into spectators at a play in which the roles are predetermined. A play in which I, by force of absurdity, am the lead.

> *'In the best of circumstances, honesty is perceived as heroism; in the worst of circumstances, as mental illness.'*
> – Vladimir Bukovsky, dissident

action!

Prosecutor: 'The defendants are being charged with hooliganism, committed for reasons of religious hatred and enmity, for reasons of hatred towards a social group, perpetrated by a number of people who conspired together.'

'Defendants, please stand,' says the judge. She is wearing a black robe, exuding a quiet haughtiness. We stand.

alyokhina, do you understand the charges?

'In his statements, the patriarch has made us understand that Orthodox Christians should vote for Putin. I am an Orthodox Christian, but I hold other political views. What am I to do?'

i don't understand

'I thought the Church loved all its children, but it seems to love only the children who believe in Putin.'

what do you not understand?

'I don't understand why the prosecutor thinks I hate someone.'

Judge: 'The prosecutor will then explain why he thinks this.'

Prosecutor: 'The charge was read in clear, accessible, literary Russian.'

The judge, who until now has spoken in a quiet voice, begins to shout, 'What don't you understand?'
The prosecutor, Nikiforov, turns red. His chameleon glasses also change colour. Sweat shows on his forehead. This prosecutor has tried other artists before. For an exhibition called 'Warning! Religion.'

warning, religion!

The judge has a neat square cap of brown hair and rectangular glasses. She sits at her podium under our country's coat of arms. The Russian Federation.

'Summon the plaintiff,' the judge says.

The first plaintiff is the candle-tender from the cathedral. She has long hair covered with a kerchief and is about forty years old. She likes morality and the patriarch. She does not like us.

It happens

She said she entered the church, began to wipe off the candle holders and saw 'some kind of activity'.

'What kind of activity?' the prosecutor asks.

'Leaping and hopping around – clearly planned leaping and hopping,' the candle-tender said.

planned leaping and hopping

This offended her greatly, as a result of which she had suffered terribly and was still suffering, even now. She said: 'Yes, it's a crime.'

Lawyer for the defence: 'Have you seen a doctor?'

'The divine energy of the holy spirit is stronger than any doctor,' the candle-tender said.
'Why hasn't the divine energy of the holy spirit healed you?' the lawyer asked.

'Strike the question,' the judge said.

> *You would have had to be in the courtroom to see how*
> *absurd the whole thing was: three girls restrained in a*
> *bulletproof plexiglass cage. All three in handcuffs (in*
> *spite of the cage). Outside, the cage is surrounded by nine*
> *(!) police and Spetsnaz officers, watching the girls' every*
> *move. Two police dogs. It's like a movie about a*
> *dangerous serial killer plotting his escape.*

next!

The next plaintiff is a worshipper who happened to be in the church. A blond nationalist. Other nationalists beat up our supporters outside the court. This is a young guy, my age. After the performance, he was one of the men who dragged me by my arms from the altar. The name of his organization is the People's Council.

'I saw the girls jumping around the altar, and I knew right away that I had to intervene. I rushed over and grabbed one of them – she fell on her knees; I grabbed another one, and she wouldn't give up, either.'

'Were you shocked?'

'Yes, I suffered moral injury and shock.'

The nationalist doesn't face the judge; he looks directly at us, at me. And I can't hear very well, since I'm in the cage. I stare back at him. I wink.

'The girls wouldn't give themselves up to you,' I say sympathetically.
'They wouldn't,' the plaintiff says sadly.

sympathy for the plaintiffs

In front of the courthouse, lone picketers were protesting in support of Pussy Riot. The Bass Player was there, holding up a poster that read 'Crush Putin!' It showed a furious woman in a balaclava kicking a small grey man. A gang of Orthodox thugs surrounded the Bass Player and ripped up the poster. Later, she wrote, 'The main thing was that

> *although I'm shy and not too confident, afraid of conflict
> and thugs, from all these events I understood for the first
> time that you can't allow yourself to be afraid, and I felt
> confident and justified in my actions.'*

The August sun was shining through the window. The afternoon was hot and the air conditioning wasn't working.

crush putin

It's impossible to sit on the bench, the bench of the accused. My feet don't reach the floor and they turn numb after half an hour. I can't stand up, either, because if I do, it means I want to make a statement, and they immediately say, 'Sit down, Alyokhina' or 'What do you want, Alyokhina?' The bench is not really meant for people, it's meant for potted plants.

i'm not a potted plant

> *If the faithful were insulted that we went up on the altar,
> taking it for a stage, I ask their forgiveness.*

'I don't believe you': plaintiff Istomin, a nationalist
'The apology is not sufficiently sincere': plaintiff Zhelezov, an altar-keeper
'You shouldn't smile when you apologize': plaintiff Beloglazok, a security guard
'Beat yourself with chains or join a convent, that would show true repentance': plaintiff Vinogradov, an electrician

You mustn't cry. Look at your hands, and silently order them: 'Do not tremble.'

i don't believe

Nadya: 'You told the investigator I was wearing a white dress.'
Security guard: 'Yes.'
Katya: 'But it was me wearing a white dress!'
Security guard: 'So I got you two mixed up.'

He didn't know which one of us had been wearing the white dress.

A giant needle seemed to have pierced the courtroom and all the air to have been drawn out with a syringe.

choke

The lawyers of the Orthodox victims of our crime wipe drops of sweat from their plump, sweaty foreheads. The prosecutor dries his glasses.

'Give us a break,' I call, standing up and swaying slightly on my feet.
'Sit down, Alyokhina,' the judge orders.

'There's an ambulance here,' the court bailiff says.
'Then we'll call a recess,' the judge announces. The courtroom is cleared, the guards bind our wrists to theirs with handcuffs, and we go back down to the basement.

A team of medics in white coats sweeps into the dingy room. I lie down on a bench, they get out their stethoscopes and begin checking my pulse, my temperature, my blood pressure. 'Lift up your dress and take off your underwear,' one of the orderlies tells me. The door is wide open. The guards' dark-red lips spit out sharp orders, and the heavily built bailiffs answer with the same.

dark-red lips

'Is it possible to close the door?' I ask, getting up from the bench.

'No,' they reply. 'You didn't mind opening your legs in the church, but here you can't?'

'Okay,' I say, and lift up my dress.

The cold surface of the stethoscope touches various spots on my ribcage. 'We'll put her on a drip,' they conclude.

The needle pierces my skin in the crease of my arm. Droplets of summer rain are falling into my body. The lines on the orderlies' faces become more distinct; the tiny pockmarks on the surface of the concrete wall reach out to me. The world seems to be coming into focus.

show must go on

'They were looking for a bomb up there.'

'What?'

'A bomb! While you were in the basement, someone called the police and said there was a bomb in the courtroom. Didn't they evacuate you from the building?'

'No.'

ugrik the real-estate agent

'Call the witness,' the judge says. A scrap of white polka-dotted dress peeks out from under her black robe.

pus-filled orgy

'. . . that's how they should translate the band's name into Russian,' the witness begins. Our supporters in the courtroom try not to laugh. 'But it's more than a band, it's a whole movement.'

Ugrik the real-estate agent saw the 'Punk Prayer' on the internet and concluded that we worship Satan.

So he is now a witness in the Pussy Riot trial. He's wearing a rumpled polyester shirt.

The judge tries to ascertain whether Ugrik was present in the church on 21 February.

'Were you in the church on 21 February?'
'No, but I saw the video. I was horrified – the girls were heading straight to hell. I had the feeling they didn't know what they were doing. For a Christian, heaven and hell are as real and obvious as the Moscow metro.'

are you heading straight to hell?

The judge studies the case.

fuck culture, we'll call the prosecution

The prosecutor walks to the centre of the courtroom and puts on disposable white gloves.

'We have material evidence,' he says, and puts a cardboard box on the podium in front of the judge. The prosecutor takes out two hats with cut-out holes for eyes and mouth, pulls them over her hands, and holds them up to the court. The judge starts playing with a jackknife.

'a snake, a stinker, a grey cloud . . .'

. . . the judge reads out from Nadya's protest writings as evidence. The prosecutor pulls a yellow dress from the box. Holds it by the shoulders. Shows it to the courtroom.

'But where's the video?' we say. 'Where are the song lyrics?' The judge bangs on the podium with her hammer: Quiet! Order in court!

you'll be kicked out for laughing in the courtroom,

Defence lawyer: 'I summon the witnesses for the defence.'
Prosecutor: 'Objection. I request that the summons be denied.'
Judge: 'Every one of them?'
Prosecutor: 'Every one of them.'

The judge bars the witnesses for the defence from entering the courtroom and orders that those who are already present be removed by the Spetsnaz team. Our witnesses are led out. One of them is shoved down the stairs, and they beat him around his kidneys. The courtroom doors are closed.

> *'If the world is turned upside down, the truth*
> *will become a lie.'*
> – Guy Debord

deny the defence

The Rottweiler strains at the leash, jumping and barking.

Defence lawyer: 'Remove the dog.'
Court bailiff: 'He won't bark if you speak more softly.'
Defence lawyer: 'It says "No Dogs Allowed" at the entrance.'
Judge: 'This is not a dog, it's a means of protection.'

'This is fucked up,' the lawyer remarks. The journalists take notes.

remove the dog

The secretary stops recording the proceedings. The judge bows her head and starts doodling.

'Your Honour, please stop doodling!' the lawyer shouts.
'Don't look at my desk!' the judge shouts back.

stop doodling

'What do you expect from the trial? What are you hoping for?' a guest in a grey suit asks me. They brought him to see me in the cell before the session. It's 6 a.m.

final offer

'I have no expectations.'
'Do you want to go to prison?'
'Not really.'
'Well, then, there's a way to prevent it. You hire another lawyer and he begins anew –'
'Why?'

'To change the defence strategy. They'll put in a guilty plea. No, no – not you yourself. The lawyer will say it in some way.'
'But I'm not pleading guilty.'
'Don't you understand that you're behaving like a revolutionary? Like a 1968 dissident?'
'I'm proud of that.'

revolutionary

'Welcome to hell,' the court secretary says after the break. It has grown dark. The stores and cafés have closed, and all the other courtrooms and their judges have finished work for the day, but our trial continues.

The prosecution: 'Not only are they not sorry, they have the temerity to claim in court that they were taking a moral stand, that it's part of their culture, in line with their views.'
Defence lawyer: 'There is more Christianity in these girls than in all of you.'
Judge: 'This is not a circus. Stop it.'

The prosecutor asks for three years in prison. For each of us.

welcome to hell

The weekend arrived, and I went to have a manicure.

In custody, you're allowed to have your nails done. You just have a long wait. They take you from your cell down to a room they call 'the hairdresser's'. A prisoner sits at a desk, and on a shelf by her side is an assortment of nail polish. There is very little colour inside prison. Here, the windows are painted white, the prison yard is grey concrete, the walls are also dull grey, the beds are made of iron. The floors are just grimy with dirt. Then here is this colourful nail polish, arranged on the shelf, and you can pick any one. Even the prison guards go to have their nails done by this girl. Once, I heard them talking:' Oh, it's terrible that you're going to be released. Who will do our nails?' The guards were very upset. The prisoner was about to be freed, but they weren't pleased for her, not one tiny bit.

I asked her to paint my nails blue.

the sentence

'Well, girls, today, you're being sentenced, right?' asks another convict at court.
'Yes,' we say in unison.
'That means you should look super pretty,' the convict says.

We look at each other sceptically. It's 17 August 2012.

kiss the bride!!

The ultra-right crowd chants, 'Burn the witches! Burn the witches at the stake!' They hold up signs: 'They danced at the altar rail, now they will dance in jail!'

'Correcting the behaviour of the accused is possible only
in conditions of isolation from society.'

The chanting is periodically interrupted with shouts of 'Kiss the bride!!' – City Hall is just ten yards away.

In the name of the russian federation

> *'The court slapped two years on them. I had nothing*
> *to do with it.'*
> – President Putin

If you were sitting alone in some bright room, you might sob and beat your head against the wall because you won't see your son. But you can't do that here. Later, you'll understand that, from now on, you can't do that ever, anywhere.

In deciding our sentence, the court takes the nature and degree of the crime into consideration, the impact of the sentence on correcting the convict's behaviour and the circumstances of the convict's family life.

putin is lighting the fires

People gather around the plexiglass cage in small groups; their cameras click, they wave their hands. Their eyes seek out the best angle for taking a picture, and then, letting the camera hang down from their necks, they look at us with sympathy. With such sympathy that I feel pity for these young people in their checked shirts. Especially the last one. He stands before us and shrugs, as if to say, forgive us for not being able to set you free.

you can't stuff us into a box
unmask the chekists

It's as though all the people coming up to our cage – every single one – takes our hands in their thoughts.
Dozens of hands are holding mine, bound before me in metal handcuffs.

thank you

All of us had been taught how to behave during solemn events and ceremonies.

> *'We were inspired by the Riot Grrrl movement. We called ourselves Pussy Riot, because the first word invokes a sexist attitude towards women: soft, passive creatures. And our "riot" is a response to that attitude. We rose up against gender inequality. We wanted to create the image of an anti-fascist superhero, so we needed to wear masks.'*
> – Katya Samutsevich

'Let's go! Go! Go!' a Spetsnaz officer barks. 'Move!' and he shoves us into the autozak.

spend a wild day among strong women

I don't have any time to ask questions. In the autozak, the Spetsnaz officers take off their helmets and simultaneously exhale. One of them sits opposite us, holding a large video camera. Some are bound to us with handcuffs; the others surround us in a circle.

'Are we really that dangerous?' I try to strike up a conversation with my Spetsnaz companion to get him to loosen the handcuffs a bit.
'Stop it,' the officer says. 'Can't you see? We're just following orders.'

clear the road

The road to the detention centre has been cleared of traffic, as though we were a cortege of high officials. We are crammed together. I feel the heat coming from under the multiple layers of the officers' black uniforms and armour.

'Girls, why did you have to go and force your way into the church?' one of them asks indignantly, making Katya smile.

'Do you really like what the Church is doing?' Katya asks.
'And the authorities?' Nadya adds.
'Of course not!' the Spetsnaz officer bristles. 'But you're young women! So young! And such a long sentence!'
'Well, that's the one they gave us,' Nadya says with a grimace, clearly expecting a sermon from the officer.

Our autozak resembles a boat cutting through the August heat, like a prow above the waves.

the more arrests, the better

'Listen, girls, don't you feel bad about wasting your youth?' the officer asks after a short pause.
'No,' I say. 'I don't regret it.'
'What is there to regret?' Katya asks.
'Would you have acted any differently?' Nadya says.

'They're revolutionaries,' the Spetsnaz chief cuts in. 'Enough talking.'

'They did the right thing to arrest them, the court did the right thing to convict them. You can't undermine our moral foundations, you can't destroy the country. What would we be left with then?'
– Vladimir Putin

'Shall we smoke?' I ask.
'Yep,' replies Nadya.

wasted youth

When the autozak stops at a traffic light, you can go to the bars
on the windows and see people crossing the street. They walk
quickly, striding over the white stripes of the crossing. You
think, *When I get out of prison, I'll be a pedestrian, too.* And
when you start thinking this way, you become more of a prisoner than a free person.
Not a single person crossing the street even suspects that,
inside the plain white van, the eyes of a convict are watching
closely.

If you happen to see a van like that when you're walking down
the street, look carefully – they may be looking at you.

6. Transportation in the 'Stolypin' Car

There is no certainty or predictability. There is no fate. There is a choice.

My choice and yours, in each moment that demands it.

'my desire to speak was ignored'

Katya goes out into the city. She goes down the steps of the court to the street. Our October appeal hearing is over.

Nadya and I return downstairs to the basement to collect our small bags and go out to the autozak.

Katya runs down the street, avoiding the journalists, who try to surround her with microphones and hundreds of questions.

'Why did they let you go free?'
'Why are your friends in prison?'
'Why?'
'Why?'
'Why?'

because

Nadya and I get inside the autozak. Two of us will stay in prison.

'Get inside the cage, quickly.'
'Not the cage, please.' I'm almost crying.
'Those are my orders. I have to keep you apart. One of you into the cage. No talking back.'
'Please –'
'Don't separate us yet.'

Four crying eyes melt the guard's resolve. We ride in the autozak together. We say nothing for about ten minutes. And then –

'I ran out of grechka.'

ran out of grechka

'Me, too,' Nadya says. 'And my cigarettes are all gone.'
'I'll get you some,' I say, brightening up. 'We've got tons in my cell!'

For the whole ride, we talk about how we are going to break the rules and make a road between us.

In SIZO No. 6, my cell is on the second floor; Nadya's is on the third.

It's October.

one road

I take a sheet, rip it into strips, try to tie them together. I have to do this in the toilet, since that's the only place where the guards aren't able to see me. It takes me a long time to tie strips together, an hour or more. I don't know how to make a rope of sheets. Why would I know? What need have I had for a rope?

Two cigarette cartons don't fit through the bars. They'll have to go one by one. Quickly – the guard might come to the door at any time and see me. Nothing will happen to me: I'm a political. Madonna lifts up her shirt for me on TV. But cellmates, they'll be punished. I'm well aware of that.

a home-made rope

I quickly tie the rope around one cigarette carton and shout out the window: '309!' – Nadya's cell. Another home-made rope drops down from the third floor. I tie it to my rope, secure the cigarettes and watch them as they're hoisted upwards. I see a hand reach out from Nadya's cell and take them. When the rope drops back down, I take the second carton and attach it. She pulls it up. It worked.

The Road – a home-made device for communication between prisoners in single cells.

Our sentence went into effect immediately. That same evening, I signed a paper saying, 'Acknowledged'.

elderly atheist

The next day is the start of the weekend. No one comes to the detention centre at the weekends. Weekends are rest for everyone – even for investigators and lawyers, human rights advocates and family. Everyone stays at home. The prisoners stay in their cells. But suddenly, in the middle of the day, my cell door opens. Two people come in. An elderly man, who I

learn is an atheist, and a pale young woman with a sympathetic expression on her face. Plain clothed. They ask: 'Do you really not regret what you did?'
Silence.

It's a question I'm asked in the cell, in the autozak, in the court-room. A question that makes me sick, that sticks like a bone in my throat. A dull, predictable question. Until now, I've answered it dutifully, going into detail, calmly or, sometimes, enthusiasti-cally. But this time, something breaks inside me. There is something terribly wrong, something unseemly, about this pompous old turkey and his young assistant.

'It's time for you to go,' I say, gesturing towards the door.
'Don't talk to me like that, young lady. We are officials, and we decide where you'll serve your sentence. We can arrange for you to stay in Moscow.'
'You've already decided,' I say. 'Haven't you?'

it's my time

They exchange glances; they turn to go. The young woman says, 'Masha, I suggest you forget everything that has happened to you here.'

My cellmate Aya replies, 'Nah, it's you who'll forget. She will remember.'

I look at her gratefully and promise myself never to forget. Not a single thing.

The door closes. 'Alyokhina, prepare for convoy,' says a voice outside the door.

an hour to get ready

My cellmates hover around me like concerned little bees. Ordinary bees gather nectar; mine fill my bag with honey. Honey (delicious), soap (I'll distribute it), thirty bars of chocolate (I'll give them away), instant coffee (I love coffee), multiple cartons of cigarettes (cigarettes always come in handy).

Aya hugs me and cries. I don't cry. I look out of the window. There are the bars on it, and beyond the bars the cold light of street lamps in the evening.

Aya makes tea, and I move closer to the window. Outside, Head Doctor Ivanova is walking back and forth with a torch, left to right, right to left, making sure I won't try to communicate with anyone before the convoy leaves. She's like a tired termite. She's wearing a convict's padded vest on top of her white doctor's coat. And if you think about it, how is she any different from a convict? She wears a uniform, standard issue; she wears black shoes. She's on one side of the bars; I'm on the other.

night behind bars

'What are you staring at, Alyokhina?' Ivanova shouts, annoyed.

Nothing. I'm saying goodbye.

'Etap' in Russian, means the transportation of convicts from one prison to another. From a detention centre to a penal colony. Etap is the convict's first step on his path to correction. This is what it's called in Russia: 'The path to correction.'

journey from prison to prison

'Where? Where are they taking you?'

None of the prisoners know. The guards know, and shake their heads. 'What did you do to them?' one of them asks as she takes me to be searched. 'No one from here has ever been sent there before.'

I sang a song

It is evening. The bare waiting room is full of women – they are silent. They smoke. They are silent.

An autozak draws up by the prison entrance. A plain white van with two green stripes.

They call us out, one by one. The convoy escort holds a fat packet in her hands – my personal file. It has a cardboard cover, stitched on with white thread.

'Where? Where are you taking me?'
'You'll find out when you get there.'

There are twelve of us. Several nursing mothers with infants. Baby boys. One of them, wrapped in a prison blanket, sleeps in my arms. He's only two months old. No one says a word. The van rocks back and forth as it moves through the Moscow streets. It stops at the train station. We stay there such a long time that I want to either fall asleep or shout at the top of my lungs, but the babies are sleeping and we wait for the train in silence. It's deep into the night – destination unknown.

destination unknown

At every train station, there is a special zone for windowless vehicles. Inside, swimming in tobacco smoke, tired people doze, leaning against each other for support. We doze until the convoy escort calls: 'Transfer!'

Then the autozak pulls up to the train, and everyone grabs their belongings.

'Transfer – prisoner number one!' the convoy escort yells. He yells loudly, so that he can be heard at the other end of the car. And the transfer gets underway: prisoner number one, prisoner number two, prisoner number three . . . bent beneath the weight of bags, those condemned by the state run through the narrow aisles of the Stolypin car. We stream into the compartments of the prisoner transport train until the barred door clangs shut behind the last prisoner.

why are we running

We lie down across one another's knees in the compartment bunks – bare planks three rows high. 'Keep an eye on her,' the convoy escort says to his subordinate, who is wearing a bulletproof vest, and points at me through the bars. The subordinate nods. They move to the other end of the car, and I fall asleep.

keep an eye on me

We must, we are compelled to, change Russia, her face is frightening. It's terrifying to live here, but you cannot abandon her. You cannot abandon the body, nor the feelings of suffering; you cannot lose your baggage, we cannot lose the pale grandmother who travels with us,

*who speaks only in a whisper, afraid even to think about
the authorities. She looks back when I pronounce the
name 'Putin'. They have crippled our country. They
humiliate and hate us. There's nothing you can do, yet
still you do something: out of spite, in vain, without hope,
in desperation. The junkies here all stick together, as one
voice they vow that when they get out they will shoot up
out of spite. You dream, I heard, of shooting us, but you
can't even imagine how strong cripples are.*

There are ten of us in the Stolypin car. I am sick. To be sick with
a fever and ride in the Stolypin car is a bad combination, almost
unacceptable.

In the summer, it's hellishly humid. There is always someone
who passes out. In the winter, it's hellishly cold. You need a
padded jacket or, as they say, a *vatnik*. And, definitely, thick
socks.

cripples are strong

How do they treat the sick?
They don't. No one will treat you; you just endure it.

They drop the mothers off along the way and we continue our
journey. Destination unknown. The prisoners in the men's compartment shout: to Nizhny Novgorod! But we don't disembark
there. I feel worse and worse, and now I've started coughing.

night

We're still travelling, strange as it might seem. We finally
find out where we're going: 'No further than Kirov.' Hello, taiga.

morning

They wake me up by shouting my name right in my ear. Mechanically, I give my full name, date of birth, and my sentence. Don't laugh – although I doubt you're inclined to laugh. Five a.m., my first dark taiga morning.

During the day, you are taken to the toilet twice. Prepare two plastic buckets: one for urine, one for boiling water. There is no food; only boiling water. Have instant Chinese soup with you.

chinese soup

6 a.m. We load our bags into another autozak, then they pile us in. We ride to SIZO No. 2, in the city of Kirov. This is a transfer prison, from which they will soon send us on to destinations unknown.

This is their trick – the unknown. This is their method – to frighten. Their way of showing you are just a body.

i am a body

They transport you. You're a convict. They laugh at you and ignore your questions about your destination. We are not privy to this information. We are not supposed to know where we're going, what time it is, or anything that affects us. If you beg, they might tell you the time.

But only if you beg.

not allowed

*In the transfer prison a guard with a dog carried my
heavy bag from the gate to my cell. His workmate
recognized me and smiled. There are beds in the cell, a
regular toilet, and an electrical outlet. You plop yourself
down, thinking only about drinking tea. In the Stolypin
car, you practically have to beg for hot water and toilet
privileges, which is why we are all so thrilled.*

The head of SIZO No. 2, Sergei Nikolaevich, takes me to his
office and speaks politely, addressing me by my last name. He
reminds me that 'we are far from politics here, and we don't
have time for Moscow's problems,' but he still asks about Ksenia
Sobchak, the activist daughter of Putin's former boss in St
Petersburg. He seems to listen to me attentively. I wax eloquent
on the relations between Putin and the patriarch.

far from politics

*Prison makes you feel more acutely that a
person is internally captive. It makes you understand
anxiety and learn how to hold it close and keep it in check.
We all know anxiety and we all know confinement.
I remember them both when they overtook me on the streets
and at meetings, when they swirled in the leaves above my
head, and when I was alone or wanted to be alone. Here
there is no safety net, no kindred spirit, and so if you give
yourself over to anxiety, it is so huge, limitless and thrilling,
so rapid and endless. Abstract, broken into a thousand
pieces, quarrels, loss of words, pity, fatigue in the end.*

don't ask superfluous questions

Convoy again. On the train, I find out that we're going to Perm. The authorities have a sense of humour – I'll be serving my sentence in the newly proclaimed 'cultural capital'. This train hardly moves, either. Now there are three of us in the compartment – or, rather semi-compartment, since there are bunks on only one side. I'm in the company of a girl who's being sent back to the penal colony from a psychiatric clinic.

aminazine

Why would they send you to a psychiatric clinic? You can figure it out. For any deviation from the sacred formula 'form, norm, regime', they prescribe Aminazine, an antipsychotic. Nothing has changed since the Soviet era. If you hear someone talking about 'humane' treatment in Russian prisons, block your ears and turn away. Even better, challenge it as the lie that it is. Because there are no words to describe the eyes of a person pumped full of Aminazine. It's as if their tears are frozen in place.

frozen tears

In one of my enormous bags I'm carrying books. At night, in the car, I read poetry. When I read out loud, everyone around me quietens down.

goes quiet

'Parting is more terrible at dawn than at sunset,' Boris Ryzhy wrote.

'Who's reading?' a convict calls out.

'Don't you know?' comes a voice from another compartment. 'Pussy Riot's here!'

a more terrible dawn

In the roof of a Stolypin car there is an opening for a fan. There's no fan, but there is an opening. The convicts in other cars drop notes through it; so far. I've received about twenty photographs. On the back, they write who they are and why they're in prison. The photographs are no different from the pictures of friends on social networks.

photos of friends

7. The Perm Experiment

I arrive at the penal colony after a month. November in the Urals is cold and wild. The women in the prison transport who had already done time gave me this advice: Don't talk to anyone; first, take a good look around; and, please, don't talk politics.

don't talk politics

I have no desire to talk politics. I want to sleep. Shuddering at dawn, 6 a.m. wake-up, I jump off my bed and run to wash my face in icy-cold water. I run so that I can find a free washbasin, but I see there's already a queue. I run in the other direction, to the storage room, where my huge checked bag with all my belongings is stowed, which is only open for half an hour. We aren't allowed to keep our things with us; they must be stored in this special room. I rush there to put away my pyjamas. But I see that a queue has already formed there, too.

shuddering at dawn

In the 1990s, when I was a little girl, there were queues in every store. People stood in queues to buy clothes, food, tickets. I'm twenty-five now. I've grown up. I was told that the country had changed, although, here, I find the same queues. The irony is that, this time, you don't get anything in return. Nothing; no food. No tickets to freedom in the next couple of years. I can't sleep while I queue. But I'd like to. Lean into the wall like a giraffe, cover myself with the spots of solitude and go to sleep.

'Attention, women!' shouts a prisoner attendant, as the head guards turn to inspect the quarantine barracks.

a woman's attention

Whenever we hear 'Attention!', we have to stand up and say, 'Good day!' in chorus. These are the rules. It is the first lesson in politeness, which I must master, because to reform is to know and fulfil the orders. Politely.

So we stand up. Forty women run to their assigned spots.

'Who was sleeping during the recitation of regulations?' the guard shouts, entering the barracks.

We remain silent. The day before, we had been herded like cattle into one room and forced to sit there for three hours, reading and repeating the prison regulations in unison.

'I said, Who the fuck was sleeping?!' the second guard bellows from behind the first guard's back. They never make their rounds alone.

a sisterhood of jailbirds

In the corner of the room there is a surveillance camera. This is how they were able to see that one of us sitting on the wooden benches had discreetly rested her head on her palm and dozed off. We all wear identical checked uniforms. We look so much alike it must be hard to distinguish whose head had dipped down. We stand in our places, not budging, and look at each other. Someone smiles, another whispers, and a third sighs wearily. Someone else stares at the others' faces with interest. I am not interested, and I don't think this is funny. Because I know who was caught on camera sleeping for ten minutes. It was me.

it's me

You have to think up things to do to stay awake: tie cigarettes together (the packs themselves are forbidden; they throw them away during searches and the cigarettes are dumped into a big bag). Put matches back in a box. Sew name tags into your uniform. Make a list of your belongings. All so you won't fall asleep. Sleeping is a violation of the rules. A missing or poorly attached name tag is a violation. A coat unbuttoned during inspection is a violation.

violation. violation. violation

'This is not a holiday resort!' the head guard roars.
'This is not a health spa!' the second screams.
'Out of the room, everyone! It's time for a search,' the first one says, and it becomes suddenly clear to everyone why the guards are here. It is not about who was sleeping. It's the search.

shakedown

The first rule of every search is that it's unexpected. Russia has known this since the 1930s, when the 'Black Raven' vans would round up sleepy, terrified people for interrogation in the middle of the night. Now they prefer mornings. This is so that they can take you by surprise, disarm you. Then they can take whatever they want from you with no resistance. So they drop into our quarantine barracks, somewhere in Russia in the middle of nowhere, to check whether we're hiding an extra sweater or a T-shirt or a dress that 'doesn't meet the standards'.

russian standards

We wrap ourselves in green coats like sacks with name tags on our chests, tie thin shawls around our heads, crawl out of the barracks and assemble in the prison yard. It's not even dawn yet. There is snow on the ground, and the wind blows up our clothes. no matter how much we wear – and we don't get to wear much – and we wait. We wait outside for the search to end, about forty minutes. After the guards emerge from the barracks we are allowed to go back inside. They come out holding small black rubbish bags. The bags are stuffed with the things they've confiscated, things that are prohibited. They are stored in a locked room and returned to us at the end of our terms, when we are released.

'Masha,' one of the women says to me in a whisper, while we are warming tea in the kitchen. 'If someone comes to visit you – you know, from Moscow – tell them. Don't be silent. Tell them how we live here. You're a political. We have rights. We may be prisoners, but we're still people. Tell them.'

don't be silent

'Hurry up, Crocodile!'
'What are you waiting for?'

They don't call her by her name. They don't tell her to come to the table. She sits in a corner, with a white shock of hair, and a wooden stick nearby – her crutch. She is sitting down, but what does it matter, whether on a solid chair or a rickety bench? Prison or freedom? She is already dead and gone, though she is still alive, still breathing. Crocodile. That's what they call her, after the drug that turned her into a walking corpse.

'Keep up!'
'You hear?'

Her hearing isn't so good; she can't answer. Her legs are covered with bruises because they are putrefying, rotting away. Her child is in an orphanage, because how can a child be part of her life? And maybe there is no child at all; she's not very clear. She can hardly remember, she can hardly walk. She's no good for anything, no good for anyone. No good.

crocodile

I take her by the arm. She clutches my elbow. And presses her crutch to her side. She tries to walk like everyone else. With all her strength. We are lagging behind the formation on the way to the sanatorium to have our medical checks. She might not live until the end of her term. If you have to walk across the whole penal colony, you get cold. Very cold.

'Go faster, bitch!' screams the quarantine unit monitor.
'Shut up,' I say. 'She's walking as fast as she can.'

> *'Nature in the North is not indifferent, not apathetic –*
> *it's in cahoots with the ones who sent us here.'*
> – Varlam Shalamov

the republic of convicts . . .

. . . is what they call the Perm region.

This is where the camps of the Gulag were, and the last camps of the Soviet dissidents.

Total isolation, hand-picked prison guards, a harsh northern climate.

the perm experiment

I was assigned from the quarantine barracks to the barracks of Unit No. 11.

My third day in the unit. They swarm around me in the evening. An hour before the lights go out.

'Wait.'

I try. To wait. This is interesting.
There are three of them – women. One is serving a term of ten years; another more than twice as long. The third one is an accomplice. All of them are repeat offenders.

'Why did you come here?'

They don't like it that I've come to their prison camp. But I didn't choose to come here. I was brought in an autozak. I stare at them. They surround me. Why are they surrounding me? I smoke a cigarette. They do, too – each one starts to smoke. We are alike, I think. Why are they are encircling me like this?

'are you deaf?'

I'm not deaf. They want me to leave their prison camp. They don't like me, it seems. But why don't they like me? I think I'm okay. I look at my hands. They're not trembling. The cigarette is almost finished. The women want to smoke again. Okay, let's smoke again. We light up. Still, why don't they like me? They say the guards aren't giving them room to breathe since I arrived. Aren't giving them room to breathe.

'are you fucking crazy?'

says a gypsy with a squint and wearing a woollen kerchief. She suggests that I organize a hunger strike. A mass hunger strike. The gypsy laughs. 'You are to blame for everything,' she says. All her teeth are gold, like stars in a children's story.

> *The world is unjust; if you accept it, you become an accomplice. If you want to change it, you become an executioner.*
> – Jean-Paul Sartre

blame for everything

They transferred me to a cell on my own, for my 'safety'. I agreed. It's November. Snow. In the Urals, there is so much snow that my legs sink in it on the way from the unit barracks to the disciplinary block, where the single cell is. Legs disappear in the white sea.

don't fall

I have to keep walking. If I collapse in the snow from exhaustion in front of the disciplinary block, I'll never forgive myself. Never.

no downfalls

'This is your cell.'

It's so dark. When I lower the bunk bed, it screeches. Like bones being crushed. The door closes; I sit on the bench. I need to understand what has happened. I need to understand. The turn my life has taken. My life in prison. Hold on. I have to remember things in the proper order. I need order.

Order.

i need to understand

'Lights out! Alyokhina, get into bed!'

It's not a bed. It's a bunk. Two long wooden boards held up by black chains. On the bottom is my bed. And on the top one? Nothing. It's empty. They took all my things. They took everything from me. The surveillance camera is over in the corner. Right above the shit-hole on the floor. Don't cry. Just don't cry.

'Are you deaf? Lights out!'

don't cry

I wake up alone, my legs frozen. I have no tights to put on. My

things are locked away in another room. Next to my cell. I
pound on the door with my fist.

open up!

Please. All these term – 'ShIZO', 'PKT', 'ordinary regimen' – I
didn't come up with them, with these regulations, these laws.
The regimen. I understand none of it. I need to understand.
Otherwise, I'll never get out of here. I need a copy of the Criminal Code. It's all in there.

I have things.
I have rights.
I have a voice.

Those women deliberately provoked me. I've worked it out. And
what to do now? Try to remember what happened. If I don't
look back, I won't understand.

First, they swarmed around me. A gypsy with gold teeth. Then
I left. Then the gypsy was there again. Then I called the guard.
They took me to an office. What was there, in the office? Remember, focus. There is no one here. No one will help you. A tiny
window, blocked up. A dim lightbulb. A door and bars. The
guard shouts from behind the door.

'Alyokhina, get up off the bench! You aren't allowed to sleep
on it!'

look back

Bright lights and a bald chief. Martsenyuk, the head of
surveillance.

'Don't worry, Ms Alyokhina. It isn't solitary confinement, it's for your safety,' he had said. A slow, soft, reassuring voice. I signed. I agreed. I agreed to go to 'a safe place'. Damn.

'I said, get off the bench, Alyokhina!' the guard yells.

On the sink is rust. No letters, no phone calls. Nothing. It's futile to beat on the door with your fists. They don't give a damn.

'It's all according to the law, Ms Alyokhina,' Martsenyuk said about my isolation.

'Are you deaf? Stand up, I said!' the guard yells again.

I have to understand the law.

'Where is it written that I have no right to lie down on the bench?'

understand the law

We know less about women's penal colonies than we do about men's, because everyone is happy in women's colonies. Women have to get released quicker. To get out. At any cost. So there are no mass hunger strikes in women's colonies; no one goes on hunger strike at all. There are no riots. A society of the willing. 'Everything is okay, dear chief.' The dear chief grows kinder and allows you to drink a cup of coffee after lights out, and to kiss someone in the warehouse. And not just kiss.

dear chief

5.20 a.m. Waking. I have to slide off the bunk and make the bed.

The guard switches off the dim yellow lightbulb, turns on a dim white one, and asks, 'Shall we go for a walk?'

22°F below zero, strong wind

'Sure,' I say.

If you don't walk, you can't wake up. So I walk. I grab a shovel – a wooden one with a broad metal scoop – and carry it in my hand.

The exercise yard is cordoned off by three rows of metal fencing; behind them is a stone wall. Dogs bark. The searchlights are blinding. They are placed along the wall and in the corners. Snow falls from the black sky.

I clean a few strips of asphalt with my shovel, stop for a bit and light a cigarette. It takes ten matches. I watch the snow cover my clean strips of asphalt. By the time I throw away my cigarette butt, the strips have disappeared.

barking, searchlights, stone wall

Oksana Darova. Dark brown eyes. A short blonde, wearing jeans and a jacket. She's my lawyer. I am Oksana's only female client. 'I don't like working with women' was the first thing she said when we met.

'Why not?'

'Because they're all hens. The only thing they know how to do is cluck. If you press them on anything, they immediately take it all back.'

She is honest. She could have spoken about women more politely, but she speaks honestly.

'What can we do so that women stop being hens?' I ask her, looking her straight in the eye.

'We can dispute the prison guards' disciplinary orders against you in court. They'll get scared, that's for sure,' Oksana says. She doesn't quite believe that I really want this court action. It won't change anything, of course, and it will make my life infinitely more complicated.

I realize that I love complications.

In the middle of nowhere

When I return to my cell, it looks like a ship wrecked in a storm. Food, papers, books are strewn all over. The bedding has been turned inside out. There are scraps of newspaper flung about. Pages ripped from a notebook.

'Remember, you can complain to whoever you want. Even the Holy Pope of Rome. I don't give a damn.'

No one else has a minder. But I do. Ksenia Ivanovna. A surveillance officer. Martsenyuk's deputy. She should have a whip. She ordered the search of my cell while I was with my lawyer. First, she ordered the search and now she's come to take me to answer a phone call. She has come to see how I react to my cell being turned upside down.

she doesn't give a damn

'How are you, Masha? Maybe there's something we can send you?' my friend asks over the phone. My minder stares at me coldly. Lips pursed, her fingers drum on the table. She's sick of having to fetch me every day to take phone calls. She's sick of people sending me food parcels. She's sick of my lawyer's visits, hates having to read the miles of letters I receive, letters with Mandelstam's poetry in them instead of plans to commit crimes. She doesn't always give my letters to me.

miles of letters

'How are you, Masha? Your mother is worried – why are you in a cell on your own, alone? When will you ever live like everyone else does?'

What can I say? I can't live like everyone else. My friend knows that, and I know it, too, but my mother and father worry. They really worry. But my friend doesn't know why I am in a single cell. Should I tell him or not? The minder stares. Fingers drumming the table top. The blue walls of the small room for phone calls. I'll tell it like it is.

no one should be like everyone else

'Tell the press – the screws set me up in my cell.'

The call is interrupted. The minder rushes over to my chair. 'Screws? Are you fucking crazy?'

The voice rings out. A whip. Actually, yes, I'm fucking crazy. No need to be ashamed of it, Ksenia Ivanovna.

'Don't you know we have a law against slander in this country? Do you want to be slapped with another term?'

'Where are my letters, Ksenia Ivanovna?'

a law against slander

She looks at me with hatred. She looks, but she can't do anything. She can't beat me. Try to beat me – the whole world will hear about it. Take your Holy Pope and the search and the single cell. And tomorrow is the first hearing of my court action against you and your superiors. I want to win. Like never before. Like no one has before.

fucking gulag

We return to the cell in silence. We walk along the barracks from the guards' club, where one telephone hangs for a thousand people. The girls look at us from behind the unit fence and laugh. No one else in the penal colony has a guard to accompany them everywhere. They go by themselves to the factory, the dining hall, the sanatorium; only I go around shadowed by a guard.

hero/haemorrhoids

After I wrote a short article about the prison camp, after I told human rights advocates about the prisoners having no warm shawls or hot water or proper pay for our work, I suddenly became something of a haemorrhoid in the guards' asses.

'Shit. Looks like the fucking Gulag.' Under the dim lamp in my single cell, I read comments on photographs from the web of

Penal Colony 28. They were included in the first letters I received from friends. Behind the colony fence there are only ruins.

chasms in the russian land

A snowstorm covers the broken asphalt of the penal colony, the ruins of buildings beyond its fence, me – a small figure in a single cell – and all of Berezniki.

Berezniki used to be a city that once knew abundance: several factories, an airport, a train station. Now it's known only for its holes.

Yawning chasms in the ground where there used to be coal mines.

the most original national idea

I examine the photographs of the chasms. There is no better metaphor for Russia than them. In my cell, I read about the Search for a National Idea competition in the newspapers. I want to propose the Berezniki chasms as the national idea for Russia at the start of the twenty-first century. But I won't be able to send this idea to Vladimir Putin's talent contest – my letters won't get past the censor.

Any phrase that includes the word 'Putin' is crossed out by my minder.

putin

Another day, my minder, Ksenia Ivanovna, comes.

'Let's go, Alyokhina. We need to have a talk.'

I walk behind her down the corridor from my cell to the office and sense how much she hates me. She holds a high position – she's a boss. She's tall. The camouflage uniform is pulled tight over her ass. They gave her orders to deal with me. She could be a stripper if she chose to. In her spare time. I smile. She would explode into pieces if I said that aloud.

spare time

'Sit down, Alyokhina,' she says, and moves the chair. We've come to an office where she can put me in my place, using all her severity. I must act like a little mouse, like an ordinary convict. Then everything will be fine. The office walls are green. The door is closed. The window is barred, and there is an aching emptiness.

being ordinary

'What's with the grin, Alyokhina? You think this is funny?'

I have two violations for oversleeping on my record. My minder says they'll take me to a disciplinary commission and punish me. She speaks sharply, spitting out the words. A whip. Her voice rings out. Well, keep talking. I'm listening. Her hair is pulled back in a tight ponytail. She speaks confidently about how, if I don't shut up and stop complaining, they can extend my sentence. For subverting authority, for example. A whip. Or for slander, maybe. Ksenia. Ivanovna.

subversion of authority

'Slander is a criminal offence,' it says in the document I sign. 'Acknowledged.'

'Subversion of authority in the penal colony is a criminal offence.' I sign. 'Acknowledged.'

'You think you're special? You're just like everyone else!'

And my minder pulls out another pile of paper.

look!

She places in front of me photocopies of Voina art group's performance: 'Fuck in honour of Little Bear the Successor' (Medvedev, now Putin's prime minister, is the little bear).

I would call this performance the most inflammatory for the cops, those of all stripes and colours, who cannot get used to naked bodies on display in a public place.

Naked Tolokonnikova, Verzilov, Vorotnikov change places in Major Ksenia's hands, until I ask, trying to suppress my laughter: 'And should I write "Acknowledged" here, too?'

'Yes,' she answers in a tight voice.

'And do you feel that you are hereby fulfilling your duty towards the motherland?' I ask.

'Alyokhina, I hope they'll release you as soon as possible. I mean it,' she replies.

do you mean it?

That neither I nor Nadya would be released 'as soon as possible' was clear from the start.

Power built on totalitarian principles cannot admit its mistakes. To admit a mistake is to show weakness, to back down. To lose.

This power sees conspiracy everywhere behind its back, so it lives with its head turned backwards, checking that no one is following it, that no one is dreaming up a revolution. This power must always be on its guard, it claims supreme power, is invincible to itself, the absolute made flesh.

head turned backwards

Inert, its actions are devoid of logic, it is cruel, it loses all touch with reality. A colony has a head official and he is the master of this colony. His nickname within the colony is 'master', and his right-hand man is nicknamed 'the godfather'. And these two men, in a faraway fiefdom enclosed by stone walls, don't take orders from anyone. This means everything is permitted.

we rule here

The godfather of my colony, No. 28, is Roman Ignatov. He's a bigshot, a major, the deputy in charge of 'regimen and safety'. Here he is, sitting in an enormous chair. Facing him, the guards of the colony are sitting in three rows. The chairs are like classroom chairs. Almost all the guards, like exemplary schoolgirls, have thick, waist-long braids. This is the disciplinary commission.

disciplinary commission, exemplary girls

'Alyokhina violated the regimen again.' The head of Unit No. 11 reads the charge.
'In what way?' the godfather inquires lazily.
'She failed to get up on command at 5.20 a.m.'
'When did she get up?'
'At 5.45.'

'That's a serious violation. How do you explain yourself, Alyokhina?' Major Ignatov asks, tapping on the desk.

nonentity

This commission is brought together for one purpose only: to
suppress. Who do you think you are, you pathetic thing, standing there in your checked uniform with a name tag and your
unit number? Who do you think you are? You're a nonentity.
A nonentity dropped in the far-flung reaches of this country,
into a circle of people who are ready to lie to your face, set you
up, sign their names to their lies in indelible black ink. To lie
without end, until retirement. Until you die.

When are you honest, Major Ignatov? This is what I would like
to ask this lazy, sleepy official. But instead I say: 'It's not true. I
didn't oversleep. They just didn't wake me up.'

when are you honest

For some reason, I still believe I can explain things to them. To
these people who are prepared to send women to freeze for
days on end as punishment for being stubborn and obstinate.
The major smirks.

'You are lying now, Alyokhina. You know that slander is a crim-
inal offence?'
'Yes.'
'And so, do you admit that you violated the regimen?'

The words of the dissident Bukovsky come to me: forty years
ago, he did time in a labour camp not far from where Major

Ignatov wants me to plead guilty: 'They no longer want people to believe in a bright future; they want submission.'

violated the regimen?

And if I accept their authority, by agreeing to lies about violating the regimen, I would be submitting, too. I'd be pleading guilty to a crime I didn't commit. Such moments of choice, made in prison, will stay with you for the rest of your life. These decisions become the most important ones you ever make. Because you can't forget anything you do here within the prison walls. Once you betray yourself, even a single time, you can't stop. You become another person, a stranger to yourself. You become a prisoner. And that means you have been defeated. They will have truly deprived you of your freedom.

to back down an inch is to give up a mile

'I will take you to court,' I say.
'You can send your complaints to the prosecutor. The court won't consider them,' the major says dismissively.

The guards all laugh.

Several months later, I win the first case against the guards in the history of this penal colony.

case against the guards

> '*"But what is the black spot, Captain?" I asked.*
> *"That's a summons, mate."*'
> – Treasure Island

New Year's Eve. I'm preparing to celebrate it, but in my own way. On the outside, people are decorating their trees, going out to buy presents. I have other presents: official papers. Here they are on the bench. I am putting them in order.

The first is a pile of the complaints I have written to the head of the colony, with her responses. I look around. The television, a tape recorder, books on the upper bunk – a whole library, a kettle, coffee, an extension cord. Complaints addressed to the head of the colony demanding these things as my legal right had been successful. Good. I have a reason to congratulate myself.

getting ready to celebrate

'Alyokhina, turn off the television!'

If I hadn't complained, I wouldn't have a television.

Now the second pile: complaints to human rights advocates about the prosecutor. Because the prosecutor is a fucking sell-out who drinks expensive cognac with the deputy for regimen and safety. He approved (in writing) the legality of keeping me in a single cell. He gave the screws their legitimacy.

alyokhina, turn off the television!

The main pile, the third, is for the court. While people outside are decorating their Christmas trees, I'm getting ready to take the guards to court. There are three folders, a different colours for each case, and each folder contains regulations and intradepartmental orders. In one of these, for example, there are instructions about how to properly search a prisoner. 'If the object is nervous, check his pockets with extra vigilance.' 'The object'. The person who writes this kind of crap is definitely an 'object'.'

alyokhina!

I hear the guard's footsteps walking down the corridor to my cell. She's coming because the television is turned on. The guard doesn't yet know that it is illegal to control when and how much television is watched. I will tell her in a few minutes. For the moment, I turn up a good song, 'Down with the Polizei!'

down with the polizei

'I came to the court for all those who have no rights, for all those who have no voice, for those who are deprived of their voices by those who have the power to do so.'
– Statement to the court, 7 February 2013

for those who have no rights

A large hall in the guards' club. In this hall, the disciplinary commission holds its sessions and punishes the prisoners. It is panelled, with rows of chairs and an oak table. A room that serves guards has been turned into a courtroom where guards are now put on trial.

I have two advocates working on my case against the penal colony. My slight and lively blonde lawyer, Oksana, and Alexander Podrabinek, the Soviet-era dissident who hid us in Moscow. The judge refused to allow me to be present in the courthouse, so I am videoconferencing from the hall. This means that expensive equipment has been installed for the first time in the colony – monitors and microphones – so that I can address the court about the ways in which my rights are being infringed.

trial in a guards' club

I stand up. I look at the screen. The judge's face is broken into pixels. The head of Unit No. 11 Nikolaeva's white braid is broken into pixels; the fleshy cheeks of Major Ignatov are broken into pixels. The courtroom in Berezniki is broken into pixels. I say:

'I can't quite see you, Your Honour. You appear only as a black silhouette.'

A mechanical voice from a small speaker answers, with much interference:

'Sit down, Alyokhina. You have not been asked to speak yet.'

noisy rights

I request that someone explain to me what kind of law forbids prisoners from sleeping during the day. The guards squirm and give answers that skirt the issue. Finally, they say: the regulations for maintaining internal order guarantee prisoners eight hours of unbroken sleep.

'But this does not prohibit them from sleeping in the daytime, does it?'
'No, it is not prohibited,' the guard agrees.
'Then why am I not allowed to sleep during the day?'

The guard rolls her eyes, and the judge comes to her aid: 'That is not germane to the matter under consideration.'

not germane to the matter

Darova asks Ignatov why the excerpt of the minutes of the disciplinary commission on 28 December 2012, which led to me being punished, contains much more information than the full version of the minutes itself. How can a part of the whole be larger than the whole? Ignatov tries to summon all his mental resources to come up with an answer, but he can't think of one. He says nothing. The judge repeats Darova's question.
'Evidently, the disciplinary commission secretary made a mistake,' Ignatov says finally.

a mistake

A report from Ignatov is filed with the court about a disciplinary conversation he had with me explaining the obligations of prisoners according to Federal Law No. 125. Darova takes a look at Law No. 125 and is utterly confused: this law deals with the ratification of some sort of treaty between Russia and Angola. What does Angola have to do with anything? Georgia, maybe; but Angola? 'That was a misprint,' Ignatov says superciliously.

a misprint

In the United States, witnesses take an oath to tell the truth and nothing but the truth. In Russia, we are only required to sign a statement that we have read the rules of perjury. Perhaps we should introduce an oath? Perhaps this would stop the perjury that goes on every day? But who am I kidding? Nothing will stop it. Epaulettes are stronger than oaths.

epaulettes are stronger?

The court takes a recess.

The guards take a lunch break.

I am taken to my cell. While I'm walking there, the girls are herded into the barracks. No one should know what is going on. No one should know about the attempt to undermine the system from my single cell. It should stay within the white-stitched pages of the case.

the white-stitched past

The girls look out of the windows as I walk along the barracks. The asphalt on the colony's paths is broken up, lined with cracks like the faces of the guards in the courtroom. One of the girls refuses to go inside. She waves at me. 'We're with you! Thank you!'

> *'Here in the colony there are many inmates who want to express their disagreement with the administration's decisions. But if one of them dares to make a complaint, then it will not go beyond the colony.'*
> – Statement to the court, 7 February 2013

country with a strict regimen

'Masha, you haven't touched your food,' Irina Vasilievna says.

She is the only one of the hundreds of guards who calls me by my first name. She doesn't shout 'Alyokhina, move it!' or 'Get over here!' She says, 'Masha'. She opens the door.

'Masha, the recess is ending. The hearing will resume in fifteen minutes. Focus.'

one of the hundreds

Irina Vasilievna has worked in the colony for forty years. Most of her life. Before Colony No. 28 used to be a colony with a strict regimen. There were only two such colonies for women in Russia. For serious offenders. While we're walking back to court, I say, 'Before, I heard that there was a strict regimen here, but now it is an ordinary one. You were here under the strict one. What has changed?'

Irina Vasilievna is kind. If I ask foolish questions, she never tells me they're foolish.

'Nothing, Masha. Nothing has changed. Look around you. Does it look like anything ever changes in this country?'

look around

I look around. I want very much to remember it all so that, later, I can tell about it.

> *'Revolution is not a bed of roses. Revolution is a battle*
> *between the future and the past.'*
> – Fidel Castro

He waits for me in the guards' hall, which is now the courtroom. He waits for me with a video camera in his hands, his head leaning back against the wall. He dozes. He is tired. The head of surveillance. He's bald, he has a moustache. Martsenyuk. He is the one who put me in the single cell. He is the one who told the three women to surround me and what to say to me. To him, women are just cogs in the machine. I know; I have heard his conversations with his subordinates. To him, they're just the same as his prisoners: made of the same material.

materialist!

'Hello, Roman Stanislavovich,' I say.

His eyes look me over from head to toe. Who does he think he is to look me over? I have seen how girls cry in the colony when he does things to make their lives unbearable. It's so easy to do: withhold their letters; make them work 16 hours a day then thrust a shovel into their hands, saying, 'Go out and dig!' 'Go on, I'm talking to you!' He can break up any friendship, promoting one prisoner to a higher position. To him, women are inanimate dolls. He looks into the mirror and sees a general. He is my minder Ksenia's boss and colleague. He's bald, he has a moustache. Herr Fritz, that's what the girls call him.

can break up any friendship

'Hello, Maria Vladimirovna,' Martsenyuk answers.

It will not be long before the recess is over, a matter of minutes. He is just pretending to doze, leaning back in his chair. In fact, he is recording every move I make.

'Roman Stanislavovich, do you know what the law says?' I ask. He doesn't speak. 'It says that inmates engaged in lesbian relations can be placed in solitary confinement, doesn't it?'

He knows that this is so. It is an old Soviet norm that our lawmakers wouldn't want to change. He nods his head in agreement.

the soviet norm of love

'And if I love a woman? What then?' I taunt him. 'If I love someone, if it's real love, you know, true love for a woman. For an inmate. What am I supposed to do then? Will you put me in solitary for this?'

He raises his head and says, 'Do you think that is normal, Masha, the love of a woman for another woman?'
'Isn't it?' I answer. He shakes his head, then says suddenly, 'But they disturb other people's sleep!'
I smile. 'So does snoring. You snore, don't you, Roman Stanislavovich?'
He blushes.

kisses, gulag!

'Victimization of prisoners will cease, guards in the administration will understand that we are people, that prison uniform and a name tag doesn't change anything. We are people. That is all.'
– Statement to the court, 7 February 2013

Dissident Podrabinek and Major Ignatov stand opposing each other in court. They look each other in the face. In my court case, a dissident defends me against a guard.

'Masha, people are saying on the internet that you are the colony's prosecutor,' Podrabinek says to me before the session begins.

I try to believe him, although I believe much more strongly that there is no internet, that there is no world out there; there is only this, behind the white walls, with Major Ignatov, with Ksenia Ivanovna, with Head of Surveillance Martsenyuk and his bald head.

the world behind the white walls

The judge retreats to her office and returns with the court's decision; it has ruled in my favour. Three of the disciplinary commission's four orders against me are struck down as illegal. After the decision, Martsenyuk turns red and rushes angrily out of the room. Both he and Major Ignatov will be deprived of their annual bonuses. There has been too much attention directed at colony No. 28. The regional prison administration has ordered them to follow the law. They have been told to reduce the prisoners' workload and increase their pay.

'Masha, come closer!'

After the court session is over, my friends from home wave to me through the court camera. They smile. They say, 'We won, Masha!' 'Look this way! Wave to us!' They have camped out two thousand miles away from home to support me. They wave at me from the courtroom and congratulate me. Because we have won. For the first time in the history of this penal colony, where no one had ever before taken the guards to court and had never thought about the rights of prisoners.

> *'If you dream alone, the dream remains only a dream; but if you dream with others, you create reality.'*
>
> – Subcomandante Marcos

create reality

February. One year ago, we were rehearsing for our performance in the cathedral. We jumped around and fell on our knees.
'Girls, girls! Do it faster!' 'Virgin Mother!' 'Don't forget the
microphone!' We couldn't fit it all into two minutes, we could
only do it in six. That was too long. No one would give us that
much time. I look at my watch. They certainly didn't give us
six. They made us stop at two. Years.

time

If I hold the watch up to my ear, I can hear it ticking, the
watch my mother gave me. I think there is something significant in this, that I measure the minutes of my term with the
watch my mother gave me. The victories, the shouts, the court
statements – it would all get mixed up and lost if it weren't for
the watch, which I can only hear if I hold my wrist close to my
ear. Very close to my ear.

The haters. They said my family meant nothing to me. Many
of them said that. But I won't listen to them, I will listen to the
time. And believe that I am right.

8. Justice in the Zone

No one calls a colony a colony. A colony is called the Zone.

Spring is here. Flowers have started blooming along the walls of the disciplinary block where my cell is. Red tulips. A prisoner who worked in my cell block as a cleaner planted and watered them. When the tulips bloomed, it became apparent that they spelled out the acronym for 'disciplinary block' (ShIZO). I asked the guard why the flowers had been planted this way; she said it contributed to the overall beauty of the place.

beauty will save the world

Working as a cleaner, mopping the floors, is a job for prisoners who have the right connections. The majority of the prisoners work in the sewing factory. They sew uniforms for the police and the Russian army. In twelve-hour shifts. I will not see the inner workings of the factory. I won't see how the prisoners' fingers bleed from the work, how they get bashed over their heads with their stools for failing to fulfil their quotas. The zone's administration will do everything possible to make sure I know nothing about it.

bashed over the head with a stool

News of the prisoners receiving warm shawls reached me only by chance. It was the result of one of my complaints to the human rights advocates.

'Did they really give them out? To everyone?' I was jumping up and down with excitement in the corridor at the sewing school. To stop me from having access to the factory, the guards had made me an instructor at the school. The factory is located in the colony's industrial zone, which you reach through a checkpoint. The school, the barracks, the club and the disciplinary block are in the residential zone.

I couldn't believe it when one of the girls mentioned the shawls. It hadn't been easy to get such a concession. It took many complaints, calls to my Moscow lawyer, requests from the local lawyer – all of this so that the system, stalling and then capitulating, would give the women clothes suitable for the minus-30-degree cold.

dressing women

'It's true,' the girl said. 'Thank you.'

Her thanks meant so much to me.

to the head of surveillance!

This girl was new here and didn't yet know that she wasn't supposed to talk to me. If they noticed anyone standing near me in the school's smoking area more than twice, they'd call that person to see the head of surveillance.

Martsenyuk, sprawled in his chair, would ask, 'Have you been smoking with Alyokhina?'

'Yes.'

'What did you talk about?'

'Shawls.'

'So, you decided to play politics, huh?'

'Politics? What politics? We were talking about shawls!'

'Now you listen to me. You can get another three years for subverting authority. If you don't want us to extend your sentence, don't go near her again.'

don't go near her

They said, 'If you continue talking to Maria Alyokhina, you will not get out of here. And if you speak to anyone after your release, you'll serve time again, you'll serve again with her. Her life is written off – she'll be doing time for the rest of her days.'

doing time for the rest of my days

There's no third party in the guard–prisoner relationship. The guards make sure of it. Because a third party – an observer, a witness, a human rights advocate – will tell others what is going on. Everything that happens in the Zone stays in the Zone.

third party

'What happens in our country is our business.' Patriots who accuse the opposition of being a fifth column, traitors to the nation, love to repeat this over and over. Who is a traitor? Who is a foreign agent? Anyone who observes, who records, who makes public what they have seen – everything they want to keep hidden behind the walls of the Zone. The Zone of Russia.

the fifth column

'What's wrong now, Alyokhina? Just sign it!' Martsenyuk tells me. We are in an office in the disciplinary block. He has brought me written replies to my complaints from the head of the colony.
'Nothing,' I say.
'Then sign here that you acknowledge receipt of these documents, and I can go home.'
He is annoyed that I won't sign off on the stupid official replies to my complaint about body searches.

When Ksenia Ivanovna, my minder, refused to work with me, he began bringing the documents to me himself. I had made plenty of complaints, and the head of the colony had to answer them one by one.

read it through first

In his reply, the head of the colony stated that all the body searches carried out are legal. Outside, we'd call these searches a gynaecological exam. In January, I had four of these exams a week, with no medical instruments or an examining table. It was a blatant means of causing pain in revenge for my magazine article describing life in the prison as 'anti-life'. I'd managed to smuggle it past the guard, so they searched me 'in full' before and after every lawyer's visit. As if I could fit ten pages of typed text into the place where children come out. That's just moronic.

gynaecological exam

'Alyokhina, sign it! Or is there something in the response that you don't understand?'

'No, I understand everything.'

'What's the problem, then?'

'You.'

'I don't understand.'

'The problem is you. I'm going to go to court with each and every response like this one, every humiliation I suffer. The other prisoners can't, they don't have the money. And you know it. And you use that because no one outside these walls sees what you do. No one knows what you do here.'

'Fine. What's your point?'

'I don't know. Maybe it's all pointless.' I felt a sudden wash of despair. 'I'm outnumbered. Maybe I'm not doing things right.'

Pause.

I sit in my chair, not knowing how to finish this conversation, already regretting the things I've said. *You can't show weakness, or doubt yourself out loud,* I say to myself about myself.

'No, we're the ones who aren't doing things right,' Martsenyuk says, in his own strange moment of doubt. He stands up, grabs the document and, no longer interested in my signature, heads towards the door.

not doing things right

'Let Mothers Go!' reads the sign my son is holding outside, after an extended visit in January. Behind him is a vast field of snow, and the white wall of my penal colony.

An extended visit is for three days, due every three months. Mine has ended now. I have another year until my term is over.

let mothers go

Lena has two long braids and big eyes. She's the only one in the whole colony who isn't afraid to talk to me. Via other prisoners, she passes me secret notes about the working conditions in the factory and the living conditions in the units. I receive them at the school, where I am accompanied to work every day by a guard.

'That November when they moved you to a single cell, they gathered us all together in an instruction room and made us watch porn.'
'What?'
'Porn. They told us that Alyokhina acts in porn films.'

There is no one around in the sick bay, where we met by chance. Second floor, lunch break.

dangerous liaisons

'They told us, see what a slut she is? Look at the kind of life she lives!'
'What did you do?'
'We watched. You need to re-join Unit No. 11 to see it all,' Lena says.
'To see what?' I ask.
'The Zone,' Lena says.

return to the unit

Lena resembles an anime character. If you painted her nails and put her in a miniskirt, she'd be an exact replica. Neither miniskirts nor nail polish are allowed in the Zone. Lena was sentenced to five years for fraud. They don't like her any more than they like me. They don't like either of us for our arrogance and piercing voices. And just like me, she hates mopping floors.

everyone talks about the weather – we don't

Lena says: 'Listen, I've got a plan. I'll bring sheets and felt-tip markers to the sewing factory. On my night shift. Piece of cake. All the guards will be drinking in their rooms. Then I'll write what I know on the sheets. I'll hang them from the windows.

'I'll write: "We get paid a hundred rubles a month."
'I'll write: "We are sick with TB."
'I'll write: "They hate us and don't see us as human."'

The sewing factory windows look out on to the world beyond the colony.

unit no. 11

In April, I win my case demanding that I leave my single cell and rejoin the unit. I am allowed back into Unit No. 11.

We line up wearing our green coats, name tags on our chests. We're going to the baths, carrying our tubs on our heads.

The bathhouse is old: wall tiles crumbling or missing altogether. One rusty tap spews boiling-hot water, another streams ice-cold. You put the tub in a washbasin fixed to the wall and it fills up in a minute, it overflows, the water splashes on to the ground, dozens of waterfalls wash the dark-red floor and pool around the drains.

rusty boiling water

There is no hot water in our barracks. You wash yourself every day over the toilet bowl, pouring water from a plastic bucket over your cunt, the water warmed beforehand in a large vat.

When you've lived in the colony for a bit, you get hold of a washtub and a ladle. You have to write your name on it or someone will snatch it.

washtub and ladle

Major Ignatov had specific notions of beauty.

'The colony should gleam and sparkle,' he said, before the next human rights commission arrived.

In the unit, there were fifty iron bunks. Half of them were an inch higher than the others.

'The beds must be level,' the major insisted. 'And clean up the mess!'

for every idea, there is a woman

We cleaned up the mess. We heaved half the beds on to their sides and, grabbing them by their iron legs, dragged them out to the warehouse. We got new beds there. They were the right height.

'Where's the warehouse?' I had asked before I dragged the first bed.
'In the bomb shelter,' I was told. 'You've been in the camp for half a year now, you should know that.'
'Where?' I asked in disbelief.
'The bomb shelter!' she yelled. 'Got it?'

half a year

For extended visits, the women get ready like it's their wedding day. 'Have you got your purse with you? Have you remembered everything?' they ask each other.

Husbands and children come for extended visits – the husbands that haven't walked out, that is. When it sinks in that their wives will be stuck behind bars for years to come, they usually abandon their women.

Wives don't abandon their husbands, though. Often, women bring enormous bales of goods they've hauled thousands of miles for their husbands in prison.

The rooms for the extended visits are tiny – a bedside table, a bed with an old bedcover, a window. A window with bars.

You can make lunch together. You can play with your child. You can sit and look at one another.

making lunch

'What's that?'
'Sheets for sushi rolls.'
'For what?'
'Sushi rolls,' I say. 'You know, a yummy Japanese thing made with rice.'

The conversation is taking place in the kitchen. It's spring. I have come back from an extended visit with a package of boiled rice and seaweed sheets.
Within five minutes, all the girls from the unit are there.

Pickles, peppers, avocado – all the vegetables my family brought me during the visit. I roll them up in the rice and seaweed sheets, arrange my sushi rolls on a board.

'Why has everyone gathered in the kitchen?' I ask my friend. She is standing next to me; we're talking quietly.

'Because most of them have never tasted sushi,' she replies in a whisper.

'Have you?' I ask.

'No. I haven't, either.'

Do you see these walls? And all of us, inside?
If we cannot destroy them

inside the walls

That evening, we listened to 'L'Estaca'. The song would never have got past the censor if my poet friends had not hid it so well. They recorded it on a CD, and at the beginning and end put on some Bach and Beethoven. Sandwiched between the classics was this old Spanish revolutionary anthem, sung in Russian.

The Arkady Kotz band, old friends, first performed it on the day we were sentenced. Outside the court.

'Let's destroy this prison,
Tear down these unjust walls.
Let them tumble to the ground,
Let them fall, fall, fall!'

'The guards took me to the office and told me they'll make our lives a living hell because you've come back to the unit' the monitor of unit No. 11 said. 'Stay strong,' she said, barely audibly, 'It's going to be rough.'

padlocks

Lena was in Unit No. 2 and I was in No. 11. There was a road between our barracks, and a square where they did rollcall. Twice a day, we formed a queue: morning and evening. In cold and heat, snow and rain.

Our block, like all the others in the colony, was cordoned off with perimeter wire fencing and gates with electric locks. Lena walked in formation with her unit, and I in mine. We barely met, but when we did – in the dining hall, the sick bay – she would pass me pay slips. Wages that were far below the minimum. The names of those dying of tuberculosis, the names of guards who had violated the prisoners' rights.

wire fences

May 2013. Putin has been in the presidential chair for just over a year, and I have been behind bars for just over a year. I have filed for parole. Ahead of my hearing, Lena and I collected all the information we could about the colony so that I could broadcast it, using the court – which we both knew would never release me early – as a mouthpiece, a forum for our grievances.

lena

Lena was not afraid of risks. She laughed in Martsenyuk's face when he screamed at her, threatening her with disciplinary measures. I wasn't afraid, either. Not only was I unafraid, I was proud – of the improvements in the barracks, of the increase in wages. We were both proud that, over the previous six months, eight guards who had systematically robbed prisoners of their wages had been fired.

I kept the records at the very bottom of my box of belongings, tucked away in the storage room. Among the photographs of my son and my friends. Separate from photographs of her. Lena had given them to me as a memento.

records at the very bottom

I don't know who betrayed us. There were dozens of women following our every move. The records disappeared in the first search after they had been hidden. From that day on, searches were carried out daily. All the women's bags were turned inside out. Our unit head, Nikolayeva, was demoted. They hung padlocks on the perimeter gates of my and Lena's units. Everyone would now suffer because of our record keeping. Everyone who came near us.

That month, they blocked the telephones. They stopped giving us our letters. They threw someone in solitary for eating at the same table as me.

i know in hell i will be

I was not brought to the court for my parole hearing. I participated via videoconference. From the club. Of course, I was denied parole. Life in the colony turned into hell. I declared a hunger strike.

When a prisoner goes on hunger strike, they have to put you in isolation by law, in the sick bay, and keep track of your health.

'You have work to do, Maria Vladimirovna,' Martsenyuk said to me with a half-smile. 'And you have to be there for the full eight hours of your shift.' He adds: 'And no sanatorium.'

On the first day, I just had cramps in my stomach. On the second, my head started to spin. I sewed for eight hours straight. Straight stitches on the sleeves. Head spinning. I drank water directly from the tap. Icy-cold water and May sunshine.

drinking may sunshine

It takes no time to make a buttonhole. Those two rows of zigzag stitching you see if you examine a buttonhole – the sewing machine can do them in about ten seconds. Then a blade cuts the slot in the centre. After that you turn the fabric, and sew again. Zigzag up one side, zigzag down the other, then down comes the blade. Shift. Buttonhole, blade. Next piece. I make buttonholes in uniforms.

shift. buttonhole. blade.

Now, no one talks to me in the unit. If they do, they'll end up in solitary. I drink water from a plastic mug in the corner of the kitchen. Someone holds me by the arm during roll call on the square.

'Even if she achieves nothing,' I hear the voice of the unit monitor behind me saying, 'at least she's trying.'

On the third day, my blood pressure falls to ninety.

'She'll work until she drops,' Martsenyuk says. 'Can't you just say that she's eating in the unit?' he asks the unit head indignantly. 'Why not? Why do you refuse to write that?'

the major with a braid

'I declare a hunger strike. I demand the removal of the padlocks from the fence gates of units No. 2 and No. 11. I demand the guards stop accompanying me.'

Major Nikolayeva wears a blond braid down to her waist. She has big eyes and a sturdy body. She is the head of my unit. The prisoners say, 'She's like a mother to us, don't you understand?' I do. Almost. One of Major Nikolayeva's official tasks is to keep the Individual Prisoner's Diaries, in which she describes in detail what she knows of each of my days. Every step I take goes into my personal file, which is bound with white thread when the notebook is full. It is the ninth day of my hunger strike. Major Nikolayeva summons me to her office, which looks like the room of a schoolgirl, and my prisoner's diary looks like her homework. Major Nikolayeva, with her blond braid, is not like the other heads, and does not know how to behave like one. She speaks to me amiably.

'Masha.'

She's not sure where to begin. She has been entrusted with too much responsibility, and she is tired. Every guard is tired here, and I am, too. It's my ninth day of hunger strike, and the press is writing about it.

'Masha, you speak about human rights, don't you? Do you know what my wages are?'

human rights

I know. I know what this question is leading up to, an appeal for my pity. Because enough is enough. $110 a month. Your salary is already low; and you have children, a family to care for. You have to pay utilities. You have a holiday coming up, and you should be getting a bonus. But I'm on a hunger strike and there will be no bonus for you, Major Nikolayeva. Never mind the bonus, there might not even be a pay cheque, there might not even be a job. You've already been demoted. You're not able to manage. You can't control the situation. You think there's nothing you can do; that it's not your fault. And I understand you. Big eyes. As blue as the sky in June in Berezniki.

'Masha, why do you insist on these human rights, if we are all worse off? It's worse for both of us. What do you want to change? What?'

no bonus, major

She doesn't understand, and I don't completely understand myself. Her eyes fill up with tears, but the tears stay in her eyes. You are not completely powerless, after all, Major Nikolayeva. But the prisoners, they do shed their tears.

But, Masha, they tell me: we don't need wages; we don't need washbasins; we don't need food from the store. Your so-called human rights. Turn things back to the way they used to be, Masha. We managed to survive somehow; we may not have lived very well, but we lived. Go away, Masha. Go away. Leave Berezniki.

go away

Major Nikolayeva's office has many books, even books about politics. There is one about President Yeltsin and the 1990s. I grew up in the 1990s, and Yeltsin spent his childhood in

Berezniki. I look at the major and ask her forgiveness. I won't stop my hunger strike.

> *I would like to live my life in such a way that whatever I leave behind has something to do with freedom and truth, and not with the emptiness that these words become as I speak them.*

'There's not much time,' I say to my friend on the phone. 'They want to transfer me to another colony. They've asked Moscow for permission. Soon, they will get it. My meetings with human rights advocates cause them too much stress. That's for sure. I know. I'm a problem for them. They want to solve this problem; they want to get rid of me, move on.'

i'm a problem

My friend doesn't believe me. Because I have no evidence.

'Maybe a transfer is better, Masha? They've almost broken you.'

What do they understand, people on the outside? 'Almost broken you.' They don't understand a thing. It doesn't matter whether I'm broken or not – the result is what matters. The thieves are being fired. Wages are going up. They're improving the barracks. The ice is starting to crack. I had spent half a year in a single cell, which is no joke, and this is my third hunger strike. But whether it's a joke or not, the results are real.

'Blood pressure 80. To the sick bay for an injection.'
'Hang up the phone!'

blood pressure 80

I don't want to leave Berezniki, and I don't really know why. The sky is lower here and, surprisingly, more dear to me. It's hard here, of course. There are just over one thousand women prisoners. They've all been deprived of telephone calls for a month. They were told: shut Alyokhina up and you can use the phone again. Some were deprived of the chance to see their familes; some were denied early release. The price of this war, the war I declared on the jailers, has become too great. I feel the tears of the prisoners every day.

'Blood pressure 70. No phone calls until you stop the hunger strike.'

blood pressure 70

Of course, in another colony, it would be easier. The story would begin again: the directive would come from Moscow, from the highest powers, to give me whatever I want. Anything I want: to work in the library, interact with the other prisoners. 'Her term's almost over. Shut her up.' Shut me up. Enough with the human rights delegations, enough with the human rights. Or whatever you call it.

earlier

'We never have any milk!'
'The climate is harsh in the Urals. It's winter for half the year. It's dark; you don't get the vitamins you need.'
'Is this all?' Martsenyuk says, sighing wearily.
'No! Drinking coffee without milk is disgusting!'
'The coffee itself is disgusting,' he grumbles, closing the door.

A month later, milk appears in the store for the first time at Penal Colony No. 28.

milk in the urals

So much has been achieved. I won't stop the hunger strike. Here's a woman who won't see her son for another three years. We've achieved so much, but she won't see her son. She is from my unit. She sits on a bench, her head drooping – grey hair in the June breeze. She says:

'Maybe it was better the way it was before, Masha?'
'Don't you see? People are suffering!'
'Why do you need all this? Why do you care?'

Why?

a loan

'Masha, could you lend me a pack of smokes until Friday?' one of the girls in her blue prison uniform asks me.

'Sure,' I say.

As soon as she leaves the storage room, another girl, in a green uniform, approaches me. She says, 'She went to the head of surveillance to report all your movements. She goes there every day and reports every single move you make. And you give her cigarettes,' the girl says indignantly. 'You should give them to me, instead,' she adds.
'Take them,' I say.

The unit monitor tells me: 'They talk behind your back. They say,

"She doesn't give a damn. She doesn't give a damn about us. She just sits there reading Lenin." Go and do something – show them what you're made of. Otherwise, they'll never shut up.'

never shut up

I do not refer to the guards in the colony other than as 'the staff'. I show them respect.

Major Ignatov invites me to meet him in a large room. This is the guards' club, where I won my court case. But the court is not in session today. He is sitting in an armchair at an oak table. He is sitting in an armchair, certain that the room is his domain, that the court case meant nothing at all. It is many days into my hunger strike.

Major Ignatov has received orders to persuade me to stop my hunger strike. He invites me to sit down at the negotiating table. My legs are shaking. The major has a red face. His eyes squint. The major speaks cautiously. Over the past half-year, we have both learned to choose our words carefully. The major doesn't wish me harm. He doesn't wish anything at all, except for me not to be here. Me and the lawyer, the journalists, the human rights advocates. He is tired, but he carries out the orders from Moscow. He asks me to join him at the table, starts negotiating.

the major has orders

He asks me what I want, though he already knows what I want. He put padlocks on the gates of my unit. He did it to punish everyone around me. He showed the colony that my unit was being punished. He put a padlock on the door of my ward in the sick bay. He put padlocks on every door I have to enter or exit. He very much wants me not to be here at all. He threatens every prisoner who attempts to communicate with me. He threatens them with extending their sentence, with solitary confinement; he raises his voice and is quick to anger. He frightens the colony, he even scares himself; but for some reason he doesn't frighten me. He has an order from Moscow, and he doesn't know what to do. He must be the man in charge, he's wearing the uniform. He must be the chief, he has the epaulettes. Major Ignatov invites me to sit at the negotiating table.

negotiating table

What kind of compromise can there be, Major? I can propose no compromise: you punished the women, they wept. They wept because of you. I hear them crying at night. I won't stop my hunger strike until you take the padlocks away. He peers at me. Honestly cautious – a question: 'Is it really only about the padlocks?' No, Major, it is not only about the padlocks. It is a matter of principle.

Freedom in prison is an understanding you have to come to. Understanding their power, and living otherwise. Not being afraid to say no to them, taking a risk. Not being afraid to be alone in taking a risk. Not being afraid to make a mistake.

a matter of principle

Before lights out, the guard takes the padlock off the door to my ward in the sick bay. She takes me to smoke a cigarette. In the sick bay, everyone smokes in the back yard: three mesh fences, a no-go area, a white stone wall. Behind it, behind the wall, is an abandoned factory. A railway – trains used to come here, but now they're gone. Stars hang low in the sky. I smoke; the guard stands next to me, I sit on the steps. I sit on the steps in my uniform with its name tags, my legs tucked under me. Night time. I don't yet know that tomorrow will be the last, the eleventh, day of my hunger strike. I don't yet know that Major Ignatov will remove the padlocks, that I have won. Stars hang low in the sky. One shines steadily, the others shimmer.

'Have you finished your cigarette? Time to go back.'

Wait a minute, I want to remember something. I want to remember this night.

Then the guard says suddenly, 'Alyokhina, what are you trying to achieve? What is this hunger strike all about?' She adds: 'You know that everyone is just fucking tired of you.'

low star

Of course, she would say that. Simple. Why are you going on hunger strike? What's the problem? Do your time, then leave, and protest on the outside. On the streets, or wherever you hold your protests. That's how she thinks. Sometimes, she says it out loud. Both this guard and the other, the one who took me for a smoke yesterday, say the same thing. This one has a black pony-tail, a big black walkie-talkie on her belt. The one from yesterday is Yana, a tall blonde with freckles. For the half-year I've been in the colony, the guards – all except one – have failed to understand why, when you've been thrown in prison for protesting, you still keep protesting. Do your time, and when you get out from the Zone you can start your protests again. What kind of answer can I give you, Guard? I protest wherever I can, wherever I need to. That's my nature. I need to protest.

justice in the zone!

Major Nikolayeva with the long blonde braid sits on my bed. Her plump legs in black stockings are crossed.

'Everything's all right, Masha. Let's go. There are no padlocks on the fence gates.'

She holds out a statement, a pen for me to sign it with. She waits. She is waiting for me to put my signature to a statement: 'The hunger strike is finished.' She knows that they will soon take me away from this colony. She knows that the chiefs put in a request to Moscow. And Moscow gave the okay. And Ignatov removed the padlocks.

'So? Are you going to sign?'

shall we sign?

We leave the sick bay because I don't believe the padlocks have gone. She walks on ahead, but it's hard for me to keep up. If you are on hunger strike, you get out of breath quickly.

'I can't keep up with you, Major.'

She turns around. She looks at me with compassion, waits, then starts walking again. Soon, she is far ahead of me. The June sunshine is hot, the air is stuffy. The padlocks have gone; women in uniforms with name tags walk between the units in formation. One of them waves at me and, in complete silence, her lips form the words: 'Thank you, Masha.' Victory. So, shall we sign?

women walking in formation

I think about fate. About how many prisoners who protested have died and now lie in the ground. It is just an illusion that you go on hunger strike to achieve results. Yes, that's how it begins but, later, you realize that it's not for the imagined out-come, but for the very right to protest. A narrow sliver of a right, in a huge field of injustice and mistreatment. You also realize that your right will always be just a narrow sliver in the field. Not there, with the majority. But I love this sliver of free-dom, however little it's noticed by those on the other side of the wall.

The major's blonde braid is a reminder of death. I sign the paper saying I will end the hunger strike. I will not die.

end the hunger strike

In Penal Colony No. 28, there is one telephone for a thousand people. In the club on the second floor, where the telephone is located, they introduced a timetable for prisoners to receive a phone call once a month.

'If we were to put a phone in every unit, who'd keep track of the calls, Maria Vladimirovna?' Martsenyuk, who has called me in for a disciplinary conversation, asks.
'I don't care,' I answer. 'Families are being destroyed because you don't have enough telephones.'
'We don't have enough guards. Do you think people are lining up to work in this place?'

'Those are just excuses.'
'Hey, watch what you say!'

After two months of intensive human rights correspondence, telephones are installed in each unit.

simple women

After the hunger strike, I returned to the unit. The unit monitor gave me a birthday card. She wrote in it: 'Masha, I wish you simple women's happiness.'

Then I was called to the office. The heads are sitting on chairs in a semicircle, and I stand across from them.

'So, Masha. It will be as you wished,' the head of regimen and safety begins.

the heads smiled

'You will be going to court. To your next parole appeal. This time you'll be able to take part in person in the courthouse,' says the head of surveillance.
'You need to collect all your things,' says the head of regimen and safety.
'So that you leave nothing behind,' says the head of surveillance.

If they are so glad, it can't be just that I'm going to a court hearing. They're glad because they're getting what they wanted; I'm being transferred to another region. Far from their taiga.

I run around the colony, gathering my bags, the things that the guards confiscated during their searches, and take them all to my unit.

'I need to make a phone call.'
'All our lines are down.'
'You don't understand. I'm not leaving here without a phone call.'
'Fine, we'll have them fixed.'

Of course, nothing was broken in the first place.

other people's letters

I'm sitting on the floor. With two guards. They are looking through my papers. Hundreds of pages are strewn around. They have orders to read everything to make sure I don't leave with anyone else's letters or any records. 'There are no records, no papers,' I tell them. 'We know,' they say. 'But we have orders.' And they continue. Bags are packed. There are four bags; they weigh more than twice as much as I do.

a gleaming autozak

They carry the bags; we walk to the iron gates of the camp. It's hot. It's July.
We walk through the gates, where a small, gleaming autozak is waiting, two brand-new surveillance cameras inside it. I get in, look out of the window. Suddenly, all the heads and guards come out. They stand in a line by the gates and wave goodbye. All of them together. Like an old-fashioned photograph of a family. They keep waving to me until we are far down the road and the colony disappears from view.

A year later, the general of the prisons of this region will be dismissed from his post.

Two years later, the general will be wanted by the police.

But that will happen later. Right now, we are saying goodbye.

9. No Pasaran!

Usually, they lie low; they don't get mixed up in the conflicts in the Zone. They make up about a quarter of the women prisoners. They are the murderers: they killed husbands or partners who'd been beating them for years. The towns where they come from – mostly – provincial towns, sometimes villages – want to forget them. Their families don't send letters; they have written them off. When they leave the Zone, they have no home to return to. The homes they shared with their victims are given by the courts to the victims' families. To the mothers and sisters of their murdered husbands.

russian suffragettes

This is a Russian story. The story of how she loved him and drank with him. Of how she grew old and stooped by the time she turned thirty. He beat her when he came home after being with a neighbour. He locked her in the basement. He stole her wages. He handcuffed her to the radiator. He was no better than her, nor any worse; he just had bigger muscles. They drank vodka from cheap glasses.

She called the police, and they took him to a cell for the night. When he got back home, he beat her even harder. So she stopped calling the police. Then he began to make friends with the cops. Because they were men, too.

my hell – my rules

Of course, I didn't go back to Berezniki. I was sent to Nizhny Novgorod. IK-2, Correctional Institution No. 2.

It was another month's convoy on the same route, in autozaks and Stolypin cars, only this time coming back from the Urals. I travelled with five enormous checked shopping bags full of possessions and books.

IK-2 is considered a model penal colony. It is on the fringes of Nizhny Novgorod. There is an apartment building right opposite the colony gates. The barracks are not fenced off with iron mesh; you can walk around them, holding another girl by the hand.

And there is also a church. A big, white church. They say that it was built with money from prisoners who desperately wanted an early release.

The prisoners kiss each other behind the church walls.

Closer to the political centre, to the capital, IK-2 was strikingly different from Berezniki – on the surface. In reality, it was the same system, just with a different expression on its face.

two prisons, two raisins

There was one other political prisoner in the colony. Her name was Olga. When they brought me there, the guards locked Olga up in solitary. Just like that. For a few weeks. Olga was a 'political', and that was enough. The guards couldn't deal with the idea that we would get to know each other, or even become friends. Olga has a grenade tattooed on her left shoulder because she is from Limonov's political party. 'Another Russia' is how they began to call themselves after Putin banned 'the National Bolsheviks, which was their name'. I came to the colony and all the talk is only of her.

the other political

'Why is she in solitary?' I hear the question hover above me in the North, the area where we go to smoke. The indignant question swirls in the smoke.

'Because of this one,' her friends say. For several days, they look at me through narrowed eyes. 'This one' is what they call me – they love Olga. They don't understand why she's in solitary. They don't understand what being a 'political' means. To them, she's just Olga, a girl who it's cool to sing with and play guitar with. They refuse to talk to me; they whisper together in corners, turn their backs to me if I stand nearby.

grenade on the left shoulder

Then she gets out. She acts as though nothing has happened. It's okay, it's just a cell.

'It's on their conscience, not mine,' she says.

'They don't have a conscience, Olga,' I answer.

She examines me through the thin lenses of her glasses.

'Smoking will kill you,' she replies.

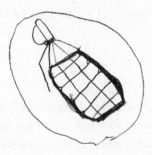

We become friends, of course. We are so different we joke that we'd never even have said hello on the outside. Olga is one of the leaders of Limonov's party – a Limonka. She's also a Christian. I walk with her around the whole colony, yelling, 'A Limonov and Jesus Christ in one package, how this is possible? Don't you know anything about history? The Great Terror, and all that? Maybe I should get you a couple of books from the library.'

friendship against the system

I work in the library. There was an order from Moscow for me to quietly serve my sentence. So they give me things in the colony they refuse everyone else. Work in the library is usually reserved for prisoners with the right connections in the right places. But I'm in the library 'just because'. I hear the guards talking about me in the office. 'We have to put up with her for a couple more months,' they say. The guards still don't like me. And they shouldn't.

'What do they have against you?' Olga looks at me, uncomprehendingly. She has a perfect green uniform, short red hair, glasses. Hands in her pockets, she is self-confident. She doesn't understand why the senior guards are watching out for me. Why this mere girl – 5′3,′′ her curls a mess – is such a problem.

5′3′′

'Stand up straight!' She's teaching me not to stoop. She trains me every day: how to run and not to get out of breath, to do pull-ups on the green metal stairs at the side of the barracks, how to box. But that's a secret; she teaches boxing only when no one's looking. I'm not very good at it yet, but I show up every day, and every day I'm more and more excited. I realize that I don't care about politics at the moment when I'm dodging her punches. I realize I want to dodge her punches as well as I win court cases against the guards.

fight club

In a men's colony, sex is humiliation. He gets fucked. He's a cockerel. That's what they say about a man who's had sex with another prisoner, one with more authority

In a men's colony, there is a strict hierarchy. Your status is your criminal past. In a women's colony, there is none. But there are unit heads – protégés of the administration and their subordinates.

riot school

The North is like the agora in ancient Greece. Everyone comes here to find out the latest news. News about sex: who and with whom; parole – who's up, everyone wants to be released early; children – everyone misses them. No one talks politics in the North. But in the autumn, in the capital, there are mayoral elections, and they are very important to me. Aleksei Navalny is running for mayor, the only opposition candidate. I talk about him with great fervour, describing how amazing he is. I tell my friends in the North, when we're in the corner, alone. We read the newspapers out loud, discuss what we see on TV.

The elections are over. Navalny's votes are stolen from him and, when I go to the North, dejected, I hear:

'Hey, they say Navalny lost by just a few percentage points.'
'Yeah, Masha will be upset.'
'Do you think she already knows?'

The conversation among these inmates who I don't even know shakes me up. Unbelievable – they are discussing politics!

talking politics

The administration does not like such conversations. And so Anya appears on the scene. 'She's a snitch! Bitch.' Everyone hates Anya. She works with the head of regimen and safety. Every evening Anya meets her in the Cultural and Disciplinary building, which is her place of work.

Anya is in for murder. She killed when she was 19: they argued over football teams. I'm her new project – the curly haired girl who loves poetry: that's how she sees me. She says, 'Musya.' She calls me what she wants, not what everyone else does.

the girl project

Anya wears green contact lenses. She outlines her eyes in black. 'Smokey eyes,' it's called. (I learn this later on the outside.) Inside the colony, I'm interested in equality and rights. But those eyes. To hell with equality. They stare. At me.

'Let's find you a decent coat,' she says.

She wants to dress me up. So that I'll be pretty. So that I'll stand out. She wants me to accept a gift from her: someone on the inside, someone who works for the prison guards. She sits on the table, legs crossed, listening to music, asking me about the Russian avant-garde. I don't think she gives a damn about the avant-garde. Or maybe she does?

'Why did you suddenly decide to dress me up?'

She lowers her eyes. She is silent. She's silent for too long.

the gift from a snitch

It is getting dark in the colony. I'm summoned to the censor.

She says: 'Let's go.'
'Where?'
'You'll see soon enough.'

The censor leads me to a brick building. Maria, the head of surveillance, is waiting there. She has auburn hair and severe green eyes behind her glasses. As we turn the corner, I see five more guards. Maria, says, 'Wait.'
Seriously? I ask myself.
Maria returns with a metal bucket.
'What's with the bucket? Why are all these guards standing around? Is this some sort of rite?'
It's twilight.

'The letters you received include calls for the overthrow of the constitutional order of Russia.'
'Really?'
'Don't laugh.'
'What exactly do they contain?'
'Calls!'
'Okay, what are we going to do?'
'Burn them.'

calls to overthrow the system

And at this point Maria takes out a lighter and puts a large bundle of pages in the metal bucket. The bucket glows in the sunset. The head guards stand around in a circle. Maria sets fire to the papers, but they won't burn. It's too windy. She tries again. No. Again.
Then, standing there behind the building, I start laughing. 'Have you finished defending the constitution? May I leave?'
Six pairs of women's eyes are looking at me. And only the censor, for some reason, smiles.

'Go. Get out then.'

the censor smiles

'I'll already be thirty when I get out,' Anya says, and she comes very close to me.
October. The people of Nizhny Novgorod come home after work and turn on the lights in their apartments across the road. But, here in our colony, it's already lights out. We stand side by side near a tree and smoke. This is forbidden. One last prisoner sweeps the area in the North. The bristles of her broom scratch ashes and dust off the asphalt.

very close

'Do you know how the Romans used to say goodbye?' Anya asks. I shake my head. I want to tell her that I don't want to say goodbye, but instead I drop another sarcastic remark about her compromised position as a privileged prisoner.

'Give me your hand,' Anya says, and holds out hers, in a black, fingerless glove. I touch her fingers. Her hand moves up the sleeve of my coat. And my hand moves up her sleeve.

'It means that we aren't hiding daggers,' she says.

If you touch each other's elbows, the autumn wind is powerless to chill the rest of your bodies.

'It means we trust each other,' she says.

trust each other

The guards put Anya's girlfriend in solitary. If you make friends with me, you will be victimized.

'Sluts! Fucking screws!' Anya's anger is spilling out.
But you work with them, with the fucking screws, I think. It's the first time I witness a sell-out wanting to go up against the head guards.

'Let's go, Anya,' I say.

against the head guards

I leave the barracks with a poster. We made the poster together. It's a collage. Anarchy, Munch's *Scream*, swastikas, lightning, graves. We wrote 'IK-2' at the top, the name of our colony.

For the first time, Anya loses her confident step. She's shaking. We go out to the square, and all the colony is standing there in formation. Happy junkies, sly con artists, gypsies, robbers, murderers – they all stand in identical green padded coats. Green all year round. Like evergreens.

'Form ranks, girls! Formations of five!' the unit heads shout.

We walk up and down the rows, holding the poster. Anya looks at me. I look at her. At her pirate's black bandana drawn on the poster. We stop and ask everyone, 'What you think of it, girls? Like it?'

The girls like our poster. They laugh. I look at Anya and think: *this is what protest should be – desperate, sudden, and joyous.*

we can work it out

'I don't take me seriously. If we get some giggles, I don't mind.'
— Paul McCartney

'Why did you hold up a poster during inspection?' asks the head of our unit the next morning.

'I thought that we lacked art.'
'Art?'
'Yes. By the way, where is our poster? Where's it gone?' I ask.

'The poster is in the bin, Alyokhina. Precisely where it belongs,' answers the unit head.

desperate, sudden, joyous

November came, snow fell.

Celebrating a birthday in prison, knowing that the next one will be here, too, behind bars. I stand with Olga in the North. I smoke; she receives birthday wishes from everyone. She's thirty. She's the centre of attention, because she wants to be, and I like to see how she smiles.

books without bars

Her shift ends at five in the evening, and I rush from the library to meet her. I'm a little late, because I'm always late. I run to the gates. A crowd has gathered there. The women all look different; something in them has changed. They aren't slouching, they're looking up and laughing. The guards are milling around, uncomfortable. What the hell is going on?

'Look!'

A huge banner is hanging from the balcony of the house across the street.

RUSSIA WITHOUT PRISONS!
FREE ALL POLITICAL PRISONERS!

This is her birthday present from the party. It is beautiful. At sunset. I catch myself thinking that the flag was hung by Limonov's party members, who are against Ukraine's Maidan revolution; they support Putin's war. But, here in the colony, who gives a damn? This evening is more important. Olga – my 'political opponent' – Anya 'the snitch' and I are standing together and laughing. I like how they are laughing.

free political prisoners

A guard is stationed by the door of the library. 'Now you've done it,' she says. There's another guard posted on the stairway. And another one at the door of the barracks.

The wind is cold. The colony is empty; everyone has been chased inside the barracks. I hear a voice behind me say, 'Guess what? They're transferring Olga on the convoy. Shipping her out. They gave her half an hour to get ready. The autozak is waiting for her. I saw it.'

All of a sudden, as always. Without warning. They don't want two politicals in one prison. They begged Moscow and were given a green light. Olga still has a year and a half to go.

'Anya, tell me where they're sending her. I know you know.'

'To Siberia. She'll be on the convoy for two months at least.'

you've done it

I didn't even have time to say thank you. Thank you, Anya, for letting me know. I run to the gates to shout goodbye. Scum. That's how the prison authorities treat us. They make us line up, chase us into the barracks, stuff us on to planks that pass as bunks, lock us up in solitary, refuse to pay us for our work. Then they say, 'You shouldn't have committed a crime.' This is the system; it's the way it works. I run to the gates and weep, and feel that I must do something about this fucking establishment, where a human being can be tossed into an autozak like a sack of shit and shipped off to Siberia, beaten to death in a Stolypin car, thrown off the train during transit.

Olga waves to me from the search room before she's sent away.

profitable property

Two politicals turned out to be 'too much' for one colony. This is their 'land' and they are defending their interests. What kind of interests? To profit from a woman's desire to return to her family, for example.

I wrote an article. I sent it to Moscow, to a political magazine. I wrote it secretly, in the library. And away it went.

family values are sacred

Women who have worked for 3–4 years in prison receive on their release a reference for one year's experience or less. This is common practice in a colony when the mandatory annual paid leave was denied to prisoners for several years. Prisoners were told, 'You have to work, otherwise you'll owe money to the colony.

to the toilet – by token

Sewing workshop No. 2 is in effect an unventilated room with an extractor hood. Five to seven metres from the entrance is a large pile of manure. In the summer, women have trouble sewing because of the swarms of flies, the overpowering smell, and the rats scurrying under their feet. The floor is collapsing, the plaster is falling off the walls, several sewing machines are without protective guards, most have exposed electric wires. There is no running water, just one tap for 100 people, but it's broken, so the women have to bring water in buckets from the administrative building.

rats

The maximum you can earn in these working conditions, even if you fill 140 per cent of the quota, is $20 per month. Visiting human rights groups don't see workshop No. 2; they see workshops No. 1 and No. 25 as typical examples. The salaries there are about $3-4 per month.

quota

Of course, my article was read in Moscow. The pile of manure was removed almost immediately, taken out on three trucks through the colony's main gates. The other issues were also resolved quickly. The barracks were repaired, the prisoners' salaries paid as they should be, the central prison authorities carried out inspections – all basic human rights.

But the image of the model colony had been damaged. Something had to be done.

image rescue

December. A priest was scheduled to visit the colony. And not just any priest – the archbishop himself, the head of the entire Nizhny Novgorod diocese. A visit like this was a big event. Several weeks prior to it, announcements and sign-up sheets were posted in the barrack corridors. There would be a sermon, a question-and-answer session – all very serious. I signed up. Public events in the colony are always interesting, but this was especially so. After all, I was doing time for religious hatred. I had to show up. To get some religious love.

The big day arrived. It began as usual – wake up, inspection, formation – all according to the timetable. I sat in the library and read a book. One after another. It was already past noon, and the archbishop still hadn't shown up. I'm sorry, but you can't just fuck with prisoners like that. I gathered my things and decided to sneak off work, not to take this sitting down – it was a meeting with the archbishop, after all! I went outside, and the colony was empty. Not a soul in sight.

religious love

The 'clean-up', that's what we called an operation when the guards corral us into the barracks within seconds. There's always 'a clean-up' when an inspector, a human rights commission, or anyone comes from the outside. The archbishop was no exception. He's here, I thought, so I ran towards the chapel. How strange – I put my name on their list. Why hadn't anyone called me from work, let me know that he was here?

'Alyokhina, what are you doing here?' the deputy chief asked me.
'I came to see the priest. To hear the sermon.'
'You aren't allowed. These are your work hours.'

I hovered near the chapel, where the prisoners were entering in pairs. The archbishop, the warden and a few of his assistants were striking poses, embracing for the photographers. Several film cameras were trained on them, and a television crew was making a video of the event for the evening news.

> *'Women prisoners produced a gift for the archbishop, a beaded icon.*
> *These days, there is a huge lack of faith in our lives and in our soul.'*
> – Website of prison department of Nizhny Novgorod

'But I want to hear the archbishop!' I said indignantly. 'The court sent me to prison for religious hatred! I want to reform!'
'The church is no place for joking, Alyokhina.'
'But I'm not joking!'

religious hatred

Unit monitors and sell-outs fanned out in a semicircle around the chapel door, where the archbishop and the head guards were headed. The guards formed a second semicircle. It felt as if this whole afternoon spectacle had been arranged to show me that I was barred from hearing the sermon. There were about twenty of them there altogether. All keeping me from the words of Christ.

> *'We bear them no malice. The Church should have no malice at all.'*
> – Patriarch Kirill, two years later

the royal night

Later. A night I couldn't sleep. I was in love. I woke to a morning like any other. An ordinary morning in the colony: 23 December 2013.

Marina and I left the North and went for a walk around the barracks. I read her Mandelstam from a grey book, a book that had travelled with me since the beginning, through my whole prison term, through all convoys and colonies.

Marina had an affair with heroin. That's why she ended up behind bars. Deep wrinkles line her forehead. 'Five years have gone by, but I still want it. I dream about it at night,' she said about the junk, just like they say about lovers in Russian novels. Marina had done time for drugs twice – she was a repeat offender.

affair with heroin

Marina is the soul of our unit. Everyone loves her. She works three shifts in a row, she plays the guitar, and sings at concerts – she really can sing; even the bosses come to listen and cry. At the point when we get to know each other, Marina is about to leave on parole. To go home to her country town. 'You'll cook borscht,' I say, trying to joke. Marina doesn't laugh; she doesn't get the joke. Although maybe it isn't really very funny – after all, it's one of the president's favourite insults – you should teach your wives to make borscht. Eventually, we joke about borscht together. And because of this joking with me, Marina is denied parole. Borscht jokes.

kinder, küche, kirche

Marina is a seamstress – 'Just an ordinary gal, Masha. That's all I am.' Her hands are dry from chalk and thread; she's used to her wrinkles. Anyway, who'd listen to her complain? She spends half of her pay – $10 – on cigarettes, and the other half she puts aside for sweets. She sends them in a parcel to her son, who lives in an orphanage. Every two months, he gets a package from her; once a week, a phone call.

i'll be back

'Alyokhina, you have some visitors!' somebody interrupts me. 'I'll be back to read to the end,' I say to Marina, and leave for the meeting room. 'Hold on to the book for now.'

In the room, I see all my things packed into my checked bags and placed in the corner. 'Sign this,' says the unit head. There is a piece of paper on the table pronouncing the amnesty.

I go to the window. Outside is snow and the morning inspection. The whole colony, a thousand prisoners, is lining up along the barracks in green padded coats. They have no gloves, no mittens; they push their hands up into their sleeves. And their coats try to warm them.

a green padded coat

From the meeting room, I was led to the loading bay, a sectioned-off strip between the huge rusty entrance gates to the Zone and the exit gates that open out to the outside. Dante would have called the area 'limbo'. But it's not limbo; it's just a stinking five-metre strip where trucks load and unload. A black Volga was waiting there for me. Never before had anyone been taken out of the colony in a government car. 'Get in,' said the unit head.

black volga

Imagine if we had the power to meet our own future. We would have a fireworks display by the colony's stone walls, catch the train with minutes to spare, leave those prison diaries behind untouched, get off the train in Moscow to be met by a packed platform; we'd run through the crowd of journalists with white roses.

white roses

What's this circus about? Putin's amnesty, a black Volga, a deserted part of the train station where they drop me off. All that had happened and all that will happen. But what will happen? Another strange life in the front pages of the newspapers. My face on the front page.

What's next?

'What is your dream, Masha?' the gypsy girl asked. She was only nineteen but serving a long sentence, about six years. For selling drugs. She gave me a hairclip, a crab with blue stones. We were smoking in the North. Putin had signed a decree ordering an amnesty. He signed the amnesty to save face in the West ahead of the Olympic Games in Sochi. A copy of the newspaper with the published presidential decree was passed from one prisoner to the next.

'I want to go on a trip around the world,' said one girl.
'I want to go to the moon,' said another.

And the gypsy girl said, 'I want to be released in the amnesty.
I want to see my child. That's what I want most of all.'
She was not released in the amnesty. Nadya and I were released.
Nadya and I and three other women. Five women from the world's
largest country. Everyone needed this amnesty but me.

vip amnesty

Big, black, childlike eyes. To her I was a heroine in a fairy tale.
'I want to write a book,' I said. 'Will I be in it?' she asked.
'Definitely.'

no pasarán!

'Well, Maria Vladimirovna, you're free,' said the unit head.

Freedom doesn't exist unless you fight for it every day. And I'm
riding in a car that's picking up speed.

¡NO PASARAN!

Thanks to:

Nastya and Max for the house in which I lived, my grandma's coat and this story.

Olya for courage, patience, bread with jam, for picking up the pieces.

Marat for understanding and Naum for a white-coloured house.

Slava for the titles, voice memos, white Montenegrin cheese.

Arsen R. for what he did, when I didn't even have money for cigarettes.

Danya for the room in Harlem, where I came to spend the night and stayed for two months, and for the work on the translation.

Yura V. for Riverside Drive. Sasha Ch. for great care and miracles.

Nadya, who went a long way with me and found the strength to 'no longer be in hell.'

Finally, Petya.

p.s.

Those who helped me translate this book from Russian to English (especially Emily), and to find its form in the first place.

For pictures, thanks to my son Filipp.

───────────────────────────────────

Thanks to Olga Borisova, who edited the Russian manuscript.

ALLEN LANE
an imprint of
PENGUIN BOOKS

Also Published

Michael Pollan, *How to Change Your Mind: The New Science of Psychedelics*

David Christian, *Origin Story: A Big History of Everything*

Judea Pearl and Dana Mackenzie, *The Book of Why: The New Science of Cause and Effect*

David Graeber, *Bullshit Jobs: A Theory*

Serhii Plokhy, *Chernobyl: History of a Tragedy*

Michael McFaul, *From Cold War to Hot Peace: The Inside Story of Russia and America*

Paul Broks, *The Darker the Night, the Brighter the Stars: A Neuropsychologist's Odyssey*

Lawrence Wright, *God Save Texas: A Journey into the Future of America*

John Gray, *Seven Types of Atheism*

Carlo Rovelli, *The Order of Time*

Mariana Mazzucato, *The Value of Everything: Making and Taking in the Global Economy*

Richard Vinen, *The Long '68: Radical Protest and Its Enemies*

Kishore Mahbubani, *Has the West Lost It?: A Provocation*

John Lewis Gaddis, *On Grand Strategy*

Richard Overy, *The Birth of the RAF, 1918: The World's First Air Force*

Francis Pryor, *Paths to the Past: Encounters with Britain's Hidden Landscapes*

Helen Castor, *Elizabeth I: A Study in Insecurity*

Ken Robinson and Lou Aronica, *You, Your Child and School*

Leonard Mlodinow, *Elastic: Flexible Thinking in a Constantly Changing World*

Nick Chater, *The Mind is Flat: The Illusion of Mental Depth and The Improvised Mind*

Michio Kaku, *The Future of Humanity: Terraforming Mars, Interstellar Travel, Immortality, and Our Destiny Beyond*

Thomas Asbridge, *Richard I: The Crusader King*

Richard Sennett, *Building and Dwelling: Ethics for the City*

Nassim Nicholas Taleb, *Skin in the Game: Hidden Asymmetries in Daily Life*

Steven Pinker, *Enlightenment Now: The Case for Reason, Science, Humanism and Progress*

Steve Coll, *Directorate S: The C.I.A. and America's Secret Wars in Afghanistan, 2001 - 2006*

Jordan B. Peterson, *12 Rules for Life: An Antidote to Chaos*

Bruno Maçães, *The Dawn of Eurasia: On the Trail of the New World Order*

Brock Bastian, *The Other Side of Happiness: Embracing a More Fearless Approach to Living*